Testimonials

"I have been using the daily prayers from Two Choice for about a year now. This daily practice of awareness and gratitude has shifted my subconscious and opened up my world in so many ways. I have come into inner peace and much greater awareness of and surrender to the flow of The Divine within and in All That Is. Try using these prayers every day, and see what happens for you!
J.M., healer, Sedona, AZ"
December, 2012

"I was first introduced to Two Choices about a year and a half ago. The information, tools, and prayers will definitely help you on your spiritual path of awareness. It allows you to get in touch with, and in harmony with, your Divine nature, and gives you the tools you need to stay focused and balanced as you allow Spirit to guide you to integrating your highest level of self, so that eventually, you walk completely in the Love and Light of All that Is…enjoy the journey! May God bless and keep you."
Ari L., Sedona, AZ
January, 2013

The concept of Two Choices provides a very positive constructive outlook, and is very purifying to the heart and soul. When we rethink our words and thoughts following the Two Choices, we rebuild our reality, we find our strength and responsibility to ourselves and the universe around us. I recommend this for everyone who wishes to connect with the divine that is a part of us all.
Angelique L., Florida
January, 2013

Glenn Molinari

Cornville, AZ

Two Choices

Divine LOVE

Or

Anything Else

by

Glenn Molinari

Two Choices - Divine Love Or Anything Else

Updated COLOR April 23, 2016

Glenn Molinari

P.O. Box 1534

Cornville, AZ 86325

Front Cover Photo by David Molinari used with his permission.
Back Cover Photo by the author.

Library of Congress
Two Choices - Divine Love Or Anything Else / Glenn Molinari
Registration Number: TXu 1-820-447
Control Number: 8204000047

Publisher: Glenn Molinari

ISBN: 978-0-9854784-1-4

eBook ISBN: 978-0-9854784-3-8

Acknowledgements

I would like to thank everyone I have ever met. They all helped me to learn to choose LOVE over Anything Else. I, like most people, am still learning.

Special thanks to all those who have allowed me to share this book and my ideas as it has been a work in progress.

Also specific thanks to the following:

Dr. Jewels Maloney for her valuable insight and questions that led to a more clear and concise final version. Also, for her use and sharing of the book and prayers.
Dr. Maloney may be reached at:
http://Ascensionisnow.com

Eric Tischler for his help and guidance in formatting the book, proofreading, and sharing his experience with self-publishing.

Personal Notes

Table of Contents

Preface

At the conscious level, my journey that has led to this book began in 1997. I first saw a doctor who used several alternate forms of testing and treating that were outside the usual western medicine 'norm'. Before then I was a follower of traditional Western medicine. As he and other doctors, practitioners and healers retired or moved too far away, I was led to the next; each one being further away from what is considered traditional/normal healing practices. Traditional medicine still has its role to play (surgery saved my life on at least two occasions), as do other modalities, some of which are listed in appendix B. Nutrition, exercise, proper sleep and common sense are also important parts of the whole.

There are thousands of choices each moment that are of Divine LOVE.
There are thousands of choices each moment that are of anything else.
It is vitally important to make all your decisions and choices with purpose.

When we reach 'the end and the beginning'
and have completed our journey
there is only DIVINITY.

Words are unable to adequately define or describe Divine LOVE,
however, it can be experienced.
Know that this leaves no room for anything that is out of harmony and attunement with God Source.

This book is designed to help you
make positive choices,
develop a stronger and more consistent connection to Divinity
and to discover your own Truths.

This may lead to a physical healing.
It quite often does, however it is best if these are considered side benefits.

I use this book and the processes described in my personal clearing and healing.

I hope this book and the prayers in Chapter 8 help you gain a stronger connection to Divinity and God within yourself.

I have minimized use of the word *not* except for a few instances where the original source used the word or for simplicity These are underlined and bold to bring the use to awareness. I have done the same for the word *but*. It is amazing how often we use these words without even realizing it.

Glenn Molinari

FREE downloadable and printable PDFs of the meditations, exercises and prayers in this book are available at http://www.twochoices.net/FREE_PDFs.html

They do not include the explanations and information in the book, so I suggest you read the book first.

Introduction

My main hope for this book is that it helps others to gain a closer connection to Divinity as it has for me and those I have shared it with. I began sharing the prayers in Chapter 8 about ten years ago and have been sharing the other parts of the book for several years. It is now time to share this as a cohesive unit.

Like physical healing, when you do Spiritual house clearing, your physical body can have reactions or go through detoxing symptoms. As with *any* type of healing, when you are detoxing, whether it be physical, mental, emotional or Spiritual you may have symptoms of the detox. This book and especially the prayers in Chapter 8 help to strengthen your connection to Divinity as well as to help detox in many ways. This is one of the reasons most of the prayers end with "as is best". Great Spirit and Great Spirit's Helpers know what is best and what you can handle.

Prior to clearing you may ask Great Spirit and Great Spirit's Helpers as are best to make it gentle enough to continue your daily responsibilities.

You may have disorientation, vertigo, emotional release (unpleasant feelings/emotions/dreams) while clearing. This is often the case with any healing, including the use of such things as Flower Essences, Reiki, Shamanistic Practices, Soul Retrieval, Inner Child Healing, Prayer, Fasting and the use of Antibiotics.

Allow the release and thank what is coming to the surface to be cleared, erased, forgiven and loved (an emotion, feeling, thought, physical detox).

You may get very tired for a few hours or for several days. If so, rest when your schedule permits.

You may perspire a lot, get rashes/hives, urinate a lot, vomit, and/or have many loose bowel movements.

This is the body eliminating physical and non-physical (emotions, feelings, thoughts) toxins.

As you heal be careful as you reduce or even eliminate traditional therapies. If you are on prescription medicines consult with your doctor before discontinuing. As an example, blood pressure medicine can often be reduced or eliminated as you manage your weight, eat healthier and learn to reduce stress.

You may see immediate results or it may take a while before you see any changes in your life, awareness and health. Divinity knows what layers need to be cleared, erased, forgiven and loved. Divinity also knows the order in which to process them and the timing for each.

There are some repeated phrases in this book. This is on purpose. The repetition serves to reinforce key aspects and is repeated in sections that may be read separately later.

Glossary

Divinity/God/Great Spirit:

I prefer using the term Great Spirit to denote Divinity. Using the term that makes you most comfortable is best.

Aumakua: *(au·ma·ku·a)*

The Hawaiian name for what is sometimes called the super-conscious/connection with the divine. It is also defined as Hawaiian Ancestral Spirits.

Unihipili: *(u·hi·ni·pi·li)*

The Hawaiian name for what is sometimes called the subconscious /inner/emotional/intuitive mind. I use the name 'Unihipili' throughout this book and the prayers in Chapter 8 because there is nothing sub about the subconscious. It may need our LOVE and guidance; however, in many, and probably in most ways, it is much more powerful than the conscious mind.

Work

"Work", when doing healing 'work', includes healing, releasing, relinquishing, 'letting go', clearing and transmuting. It only includes 'curing' of physical symptoms and ailments if they are no longer needed for soul growth and spiritual development. If you are working on physical, emotional or mental symptoms make sure you remember the previous sentence. Keep enjoyment in the process.

Even though the Unihipili (see Chapter 5) is much more powerful than the conscious mind, it is in many ways like a three or four year old child. It needs guidance and LOVE. It also likes to investigate. The Unihipili, or child within, will respond or react according to your "choice". The Unihipili, like children, dislikes work and likes to play, therefore I use the word carefully when doing any kind of healing, releasing and transmuting.

Uhane: *(u·ha·ne)*

The Hawaiian name for what is sometimes called the consciousness/waking/rational mind.

love: (lower case denotes human love as defined in the dictionary)

Is often defined as: feel affection for, adore, worship, be in love with, be devoted to, care for, find irresistible, be keen on and be fond of. This kind of love leaves room for judgment, anger, attachment, jealousy and other negative thoughts and feelings/emotions that are of a lower vibrational frequency.

Divine LOVE: (all upper case denotes Divine LOVE)

The word or phrase, is basically indefinable, except to Know it leaves no room for anything that is out of harmony and attunement with God Source.

Violet Flame:

Some people have asked or wondered what the 'Violet Flame' is. Several definitions combined into one is that the Violet Flame is the essence of a unique Spiritual light, which has the qualities of mercy, forgiveness, freedom and transmutation.

Transmutation:

The dictionary definition is change/alteration/ transformation/metamorphosis.

As used in this book, transmutation is one of Divinity's tools for changing what is often referred to as dark/negative/evil into LOVE and LIGHT.

Healing, Transmuting, Releasing and Integrating:

Any time any form of the words *heal, clear* or *release* is used in a clearing or healing it includes the process of healing the energetic causes, transmuting any 'negative' into its 'positive' and Loving counterpart, releasing the unhealthy attachments and integrating the positive, life affirming and Loving aspects into yourself. If you have a pain, discomfort, injury or disease treat it at the physical level with physical means. It is always a good idea to also treat the pain, discomfort, injury or disease by Healing, Transmuting, Releasing and Integrating at the spiritual, mental and emotional levels as well.

"As is best":

Many of my prayers, the way I say them, are finished with "as is best". This is my way of turning the prayer or request over to Great Spirit/God/Divinity without attachment to a desired outcome or an expectation. If you have another way of turning it over to Great Spirit use your way. Just make sure you turn it over. Also, remember you are responsible to do your part. If you sit on the couch and eat or drink all day and pray, "make me healthy" or "make me wealthy", do you really expect to be made healthy or wealthy.

Feelings and Emotions:

There is such a fine line between the definitions of 'feeling' 'and emotion' that they can be easily confused. In many dictionaries one word is used to define the other. I understand feelings as held inside and often unexpressed, and emotions as expressed feelings, both literally and nonverbally. As an example, if you feel angry at someone **but** put on a happy face, that is a feeling. If you express the feeling outwardly that is an emotion. An emotion is the outward expression of a feeling. This is how I use the words in this book. Most places you will see 'feelings/emotions' rather than as separate words, since they are healed and released in the same way.

Co-Creation and Manifesting:

To me there is a difference between 'co-creation' with Great Spirit and 'manifestation'. Co-creation is more at the spiritual and energetic level and Manifestation is more at the physical and human action level.

Entity:

Everything, everyone, every human, every non-human, every spirit, and each and every awareness, what we perceive and describe as Light and what we perceive and describe as Dark, is an entity. As an example, all of the following are entities: the earth, a rock, a grain of sand, a street sign, each hair on our heads, each molecule that makes up our hair, each atom that makes up the molecule, each proton, electron and neutron. The energies that make up all of these things are entities. This can be expanded in all directions infinitely.

Judgment and Non-judgmental:

I use 'non-judgmental' as meaning **allowing** the other person or Being their own path, free will, truths and perceptions. A decision based on an objective observation is different than a 'judgment' and more like assessment. With objective assessment you can then take the appropriate action or inaction.

Accept, Accepting and Acceptance:

Rather than using the word non-judgmental it is more potent, more clear and more uplifting to say "unconditionally accepting" or "unconditional acceptance". This is at spiritual and energetic levels to allow others their own perceptions, choices and realities. It is appropriate and wise to protect yourself from any kind of abuse or mistreatment, whether verbal, physical or very subtle. If someone or an organization is abusing or mistreating you in anyway, distance yourself from them energetically **and** physically if you are able. If you are **temporarily** in a position where you are physically 'trapped', use a method to prevent taking on the energy as a personal belief . Acceptance is different than accepting negative people or circumstances into your life. It refers primarily to your feelings, as they are, relative to the negative people or circumstances. See Yourself as safe.

Remember to unconditionally accept your self.

Compassion - As We Have Been Taught By Society And The Dictionary:

sorrow for the sufferings or trouble of another or others, with the urge to help; pity; deep sympathy; the feeling of empathy for others; emotion that we feel in response to the suffering of others that motivates a desire to help; suffering together with another; participation in suffering; requires walking with the other person and feeling with them their suffering; deep awareness of the suffering of another coupled with the wish to relieve it. This version of compassion defines someone as a victim and is thus a form of judgment.

Compassion - Higher Dimensional Version Of:

Deep awareness of the suffering of another without the need to relieve it, feeling total appreciation for its value; a state of unconditional acceptance and LOVE.

Accept that each person is choosing their problem(s) and have to connect with their own Higher SELF in order to heal;

We must shift our perspective of compassion and begin using a version that is beyond what we have been taught. We must move into the realm of unconditional acceptance, leaving pity and the need to 'fix' behind.

We must suspend all judgment of the actions of another. We must be aware of those actions, how painful they are and at the same time realize that they have a value and that this value pertains to the role they play in facilitating our spiritual growth as souls

Power - Dictionary Definition:

Authority, control, influence, supremacy, command, dominance, force.

Manipulation would be the key word; the power to manipulate situations and those around you.

Power - As Used In This Book:

Personal power comes from wisdom. Real personal power is a subtle quality of Beingness rather than a force.

Real power has nothing to do with control, especially the control of others. Conversely, real power is surrendering to the highest good.

Real power naturally settles within one's Beingness of its own accord as Wisdom and Love increase.

Wisdom - Dictionary Definition:

Understanding, knowledge, intelligence, accumulated learning, opinion widely held, accumulated philosophic or scientific learning, the judicious application of knowledge.

Wisdom - As Used In This Book

Wisdom has nothing to do with the level of one's attained knowledge, age, intelligence or I.Q. rating. Wisdom is born of LOVE arising from the heart. Wisdom becomes part of your Being.

Some aspects of wisdom: Acceptance, Patience and Perseverance, Attitude, Silence, Personal Responsibility, Gentleness and Serenity, Value and Priorities, and Respect

True Wisdom is beyond words and the intellect, and is only fully understood by the heart through Awareness.

To understand wisdom as clearly as possible with the intellect, the main aspects of wisdom also need to be understood. These are expanded on in my second book; *Awareness - A Path To Spiritual and Physical Health And Well-Being.*

"Amen" at the end of prayers

How many of us have said the word "Amen" at the end of a prayer without really giving it a second thought? Have you ever said "Amen" , without thought, as a ratification of what is said? You may be saying, "May it be done as the speaker has prayed". Did you fully understand the prayer and did you fully agree with it?

As regards the etymology, which is the study of the origins of words, many believe "Amen" is a derivative from the Hebrew verb *aman* "to strengthen" or "confirm". Some believe the word was originally derived from a Sanskrit word "aum", meaning "to sound out loudly" and some believe it simply means "truly" or "so be it". Is it simply a form of affirmation or confirmation of the speaker's own thought?

In forms of worship a final amen, as now used, often sums up and confirms a prayer.

In many cases the word "Amen" is used as nothing more than a formula of conclusion —*finis,* indicating that the statement or prayer is ended and completed.

The seeming ambiguity of the word "Amen" is why I finish my prayers with "As is best" and "Thank you".

Stealing:

It is best never to steal. I'll leave it to you to decide if stealing a loaf of bread when one is literally starving is in Harmony with LOVE. It is best to ask for what one needs.

Breaking Promises:

It is best never to break a promise (unless it was made in anger or spite). If you do your best to keep your promise and a flat tire or true emergency interferes, explain and apologize.

Lying:

It is best never to lie. I'll leave it to you to decide if telling someone, "I forgot to buy your birthday present", is in Harmony with LOVE when you bought the present and want to surprise them.

Even though these are 'my' definitions, I hope they are thought-provoking for you. Think for yourself.

Personal Notes

Chapter 1

GOD IS...

This will be a very short Chapter.

Use whichever word for God that makes you comfortable; God, Great Spirit, Divinity or Oneness are a few that may allow you to feel the greatest comfort without an attempt to define.

ANY attempt on our part to describe or define God is limiting.

I prefer to use the term Great Spirit, so, I will be using that term most often.

Before reading the rest of the book I strongly suggest reading the glossary. This will help to clarify my use of certain terms and words and allow you to reword as you wish when I use those terms.

Personal Notes

Chapter 2
Divine LOVE vs. love

Practicing Divine LOVE to the best of our abilities is the single most important practice each of us, individually and collectively, can do in order to get closer to God Source. Remember this includes LOVING yourself.

It is acceptable and appropriate to love other beings, music, food and even material objects.

Divine LOVE:

Words are unable to adequately define or describe Divine LOVE. Rather it is an experience. Know that LOVE leaves no room for anything that is out of harmony or attunement with God Source.

love as most people define it:

feel affection for,
adore,
worship,
be in love with,
romance,
be devoted to,
care for,
find irresistible,
be keen on and
be fond of.

These definitions of love leave room for judgment, anger, jealousy, attachments and other thoughts and feelings/emotions that are of something other than Divine LOVE.

As long as we are in human body the ego is needed. It needs to be strongly focused and well disciplined through LOVING use of both the conscious mind and the Unihipili (subconscious mind). The presence and correct functioning of the mind/ego aspect of ourselves is essential in achieving a harmonious balance between the different levels of self. Everything begins with thought and intention.

Personal Notes

Chapter 3

From Battle To Forgiveness To LOVE

Most people have been doing battle, at least occasionally, as a person in a human body and/or as an entity in the unmanifest realms. The concept of battle is simple. Any time one is vanquishing, conquering, defeating, crushing, annihilating, killing, overcoming and/or overpowering any person, being, entity or something 'bad' or 'wrong', that person is in battle. If one is in battle he or she may need to continue in battle for a time while they begin to practice forgiving and LOVING. The more you can let go of battle and practice Forgiveness and Unconditional LOVE, the stronger the connection to and guidance and protection from Great Spirit.

Some people believe there is no need to get in touch with the form of their anger and guilt that is symbolized for them in some way; that they simply need to forgive. Other people believe that you always have to completely understand the roots of your anger, discomfort, guilt, doubt, memories replaying, trapped emotions or suppressed feelings and emotions. Perhaps whichever way works for you is appropriate and will get you well on your way. Quite often a short prayer and LOVE will clear 'things'. Other times more conscious knowing may be needed. Simply ask, "is it best that I know more?", and keep investigating until there is no more conscious knowing needed. Then heal and release with LOVE.

To begin the shift, just do your best.

If you feel there is no need to forgive or feel that something or someone is unforgivable, say mentally, "I forgive", with as much conviction as you are willing to muster at the time. Great Spirit and Great Spirit helpers begin to take care of the rest and you will begin to shift further into forgiveness and LOVE. Most of this LOVING and forgiving is done silently.

At some point, if you are practicing as best as you can, you will realize you are less angry and the shift towards forgiveness and LOVE becomes less hidden.

Eventually you will Know and be fully aware that there is only LOVE and all else is to help us get to that Knowingness and Oneness.

It does take perseverance and practice.

LOVE is reached by your entire Being. Continue to do your best.

Instead of engaging the ego and what you perceive as negative or dark, send it Divine LOVE and LIGHT.

In time, you will access your own ability to root out the sources of your resistance. How did they come about? What agreements from your history allowed them? What learned beliefs are limiting you? What unhealthy feelings/emotions are affecting you? These can all be cleared and healed with LOVE. Many who have been working with their shadow aspects and/or with what they consider to be demons or dark spirits have been in battle. Debbie Ford brought forth excellent ways to work with the shadow without battle.

Below is adapted from *The Dark Side of the Light Chasers by* Debbie Ford.

The reason we do shadow work is to become whole. Un-conceal, love, and embrace your shadow as well as your light, including your light shadow (those qualities you see in others), **but** do **not** own yourself. It is your birthright to be whole: to have it all. It only takes a shift in perception and an opening of the heart. When you can say "I am That" to the deepest, darkest parts of yourself (that have been disowned), then you can reach enlightenment.

Embracing our shadow and our light takes us to a new place in consciousness where we have to open our hearts to all of ourselves, and to all of humanity. Every aspect of ourselves has a gift; and every aspect of you, whether you like it or not, can and will benefit your life. There is light in every part of us and in all of the universe: the universe is within you. When we embrace all of it, we find and feel the extraordinary design of life.

We're taught never to say negative things about ourselves. If I wake up feeling worthless, I'm supposed to pretend that I do**n't** feel that way. I'm supposed to tell myself I am worthy and hope I will come to feel worthy later in the day, or sometime in this lifetime! I have to go to work, or out among the world pretending to feel worthy. I have to hide behind my mask of worthiness all day, hoping no one will see through it. **But** inside, I feel a quiet despair knowing that I am **not** being myself, all because I'm unable to embrace being worthless. We often resist this aspect of ourselves and pass judgments on this kind of person we perceive as worthless.

When we integrate negative traits, we no longer need affirmations because we *Know* that we're both worthy and worthless, ugly and beautiful, lazy and conscientious. When we only believe we can be one or the other, we continue our internal struggle to only be the 'right' things. When we believe we are weak, nasty, selfish, unenlightened - traits that we often believe our family and friends do**n't** possess - we feel shame. When we believe or pretend we are only worthy, conscientious, caring, loving and so on, we are denying and repressing the parts we believe to be 'dark', thus denying ourselves our wholeness. When you own ALL the traits of the universe and humankind, you'll understand that every single trait has something to teach you (a gift) and all of these teachers, 'dark' and 'light', will give you access to all the wisdom of the world. Ford, Debbie. (1998). *The Dark Side Of The Light Chasers.* New York: The Berkley Publishing Group.

Many people, including those in the 'New Age' community have been busy battling demons, thinking that demons are outside themselves. Jed McKenna, author of Spiritual Warfare has an excellent conception of what demons and dark spirits are really all about.

Below is adapted from *Spiritual Warfare* by Jed McKenna pages 258-261

> If you've made your peace, then the devils are really angels freeing
> you from the earth..

You all know what it's like to have a critical voice in your head? Some person or thought or emotion that has taken up residence in your head and tends to be a bit on the obnoxious side?.

Well, those are demons. Demon is a useful way to describe anything in our heads that we do**n't** want there and which seems to have a mind of its own; something that haunts us or has power over us (memories, people, addictions). They torment us in a variety of ways. The main thing demons do is hold us back, restrict our progress.

Imagine you're climbing out of a dark sewer and some beast has its teeth sunk into your leg, making a lot of noise and tearing at you and weighing you down; a demon. Are you going to jump back down into the sewer and fight it? A lot of people think that's the answer, **but** why do that? It's tough to slay demons because they're symptoms, **not** causes, and even if you kill one, there are always more. What's next, a fight to the death with your obsessive neatness? Pistols at dawn with your love of chocolate? The only real result of these little battles is that you have**n't** gone anywhere; you're still in the sewer. All you've really killed is time, and time is all you really have. You have**n't** killed a demon, you've lost a piece of your life, and that means they've won; the part of you that's afraid to move forward has won. You have to ask yourself, what's your objective? To slay every little demon or to rise up out of the realms they inhabit?

It seems that most people seek solutions within the sewer rather than escape from it.

Battling demons is the ultimate form of shadow boxing. You're just punching at an empty projection of yourself. For our purposes, if demons are**n't** demonizing you, then they do**n't** exist. It is as simple as that.

Even though this may seem like a cop out, dealing with our issues is the real cop out. It's our way of avoiding the real war by engaging ourselves at the level of minor skirmishes.

As we develop a subtler and more refined understanding of what a demon is, identifying them by what they do, **not** how they look, we begin to see that demons are**n't** limited to addictions and critical voices. It's **not** just negative attachments that hold us captive within ego's sphere, it's all attachments. The approach to life and spirituality where we decrease bad things like sins and addictions, and increase good things like love and compassion, never has and never will move anyone a single step in the direction of awakening.

For example, if you have an addiction (gambling, smoking, alcohol, sex, watching TV, exercise), then a large portion of your life energy - your time, your thoughts and emotions - would be spent either partaking of the addiction or fighting your urge to partake of the activity. For our purposes feeding your addiction and fighting it are really the same. Whether your addiction demon is beating you or you are beating it does**n't** matter, all that matters is that you are sitting in your prison cell fully engaged in processes that will never move you one inch closer to liberation. That's what demons do. They're like Maya's army of winged monkeys. They always fight a delaying action that expends our resources and prevents us from making forward progress. That's their objective, to occupy us, **not** to defeat us.

Say, for instance, that after twenty years of fighting your addiction, you finally manage to overcome it. What would you have to show for that victory?

Twenty years gone.

Demons keep us unfocused and distracted. The need to deal with tormenting demons comes up again and again as we progress, so you have to know what to do as a matter of policy; keep climbing or jump down and fight? My advice: Fight when you have to, climb when you can. Further is everything.

Is it possible that these demons could be used in a positive way? Is there any way demons might be useful? McKenna, Jed. (2007). *Spiritual Warfare.* WiseFool Press: (p. 258-261)

Jed McKenna's answer to the two questions above is yes. He has a two or three page answer that makes sense to me and at the same time is confusing.

My answer is also yes. I feel that demons and nasty people give us a chance to choose LOVE or Anything Else.

What is Anything Else? Fear... Of course! Fear disguised as love. Fear disguised as morality. Fear disguised as compassion and helping others. Fear making the unreal seem real. The animal part of us that is designed to survive, to protect our young and to keep our species going needs appropriate fears. However fear can drive the whole process until we go beyond inappropriate fear. We can become stuck in fear that has nothing to do with survival.

The two polarities of positive (as used to indicate Love, humility, kindness) and negative (arrogance, impatience, anger, fear, greed) need to be balanced and integrated. The great power of the negative is transformed by the positive and the positive is grounded by its relationship to the negative.

Chapter 4

Choices

and How They Affect You, Your Energy Centers and All That Is

Recognizing Choices As Love Or Anything Else.

Thoughts, words and actions become habits, either positively charged or negatively charged.

As a General Rule:

Many small lies and/or a few large lies might end a relationship and may center you in a lower energy field for an undetermined amount of time.

One or more broken promises might end a relationship and may center you in a lower energy field for an undetermined amount of time.

Stealing will end a friendship quickly and may center you in a lower energy field quickly for an undetermined amount of time.

Positive or negative thoughts, words and actions pull you towards a more positive or negative energy field and attract those energies to you.

This affects and shifts "A Momentum Tunnel" and without conscious intent you tend to continue on the same path.

This also affects the universal energy and vibrational frequency of mankind and the Universe.

The Universe only understands "yes". It is critical to use the positive counterpart of any negative. If you say, "I will not be Angry" or "I am not angry", the Universe hears, "I will be angry" or "I am angry". Instead say, "I will be forgiving, LOVING" or "I am forgiving, LOVING" (unconditional love). If you have difficulty thinking of an appropriate word, use the positive word or words that come the closest. Interestingly, when you think or say, "I am not happy", the universe keeps the 'not' in place and energizes the opposite of happy. Be mindful of how you think and speak.
The following may help you to recognize choices as Love or Anything Else and thus help you to shift your energy.

Remember LOVE		All Are Choices Anything Else
Courage, LOVE and Positive Thoughts	**or**	**Fear**
Truth	**or**	**Lies**
Promise kept	**or**	**Promises broken**
Honoring what belongs to others	**or**	**Stealing**
A kind/positive thought	**or**	**An angry/negative/unkind thought**
A kind/positive word	**or**	**An angry/negative/unkind word**
A kind/positive action	**or**	**An angry/negative/unkind action**
Forgiving/accepting/Loving	**or**	**Judging/unforgiving/hate/prejudice**
Allowing others their beliefs	**or**	**Trying to impose your beliefs on others**
Allowing others their life style		**Trying to control or manipulate others**
Etc.	**or**	**Etc.**

Stealing:

It is best never to steal. I'll leave it to you to decide if stealing a loaf of bread when one is literally starving is in Harmony with LOVE. It is best to ask for what one needs.

Breaking Promises:

It is best never to break a promise (unless it was made in anger or spite). If you do your best to keep your promise and a flat tire or true emergency interferes, explain and apologize.

Lying:

It is best never to lie. I'll leave it to you to decide if telling someone, "I forgot to buy your birthday present", is in Harmony with LOVE when you bought the present and want to surprise them.

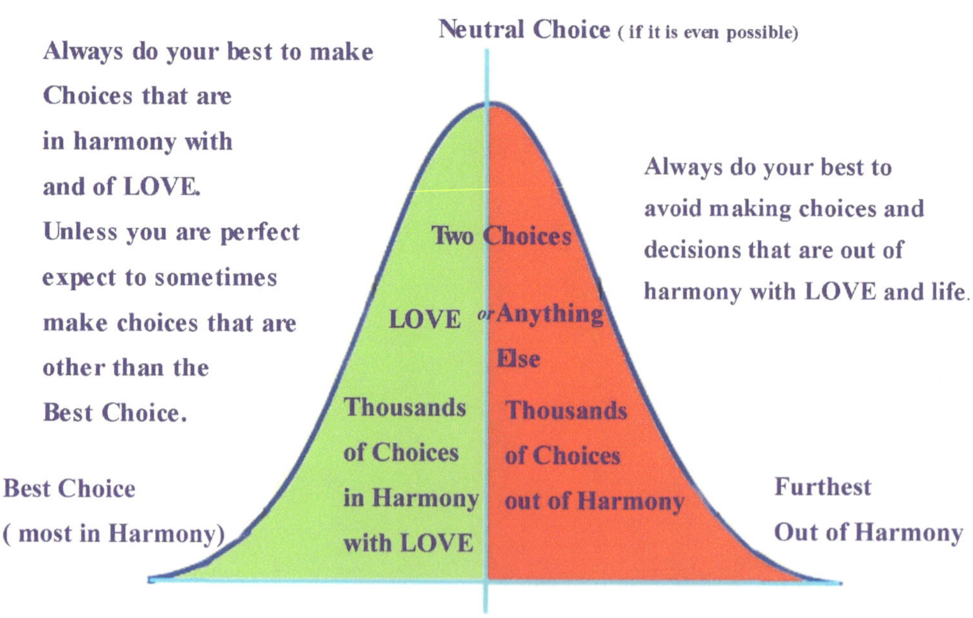

How Choices affect the Seven most commonly known Chakras

Physical and psychological problems have their source in negative thought forms. Unfavorable thoughts often begin in the conscious mind even if you are unaware of them and are then held in the subconscious mind. The thought may have begun in the conscious mind earlier in this life or in a previous life. Through the subconscious they then affect the physical body. The body can also be healed with favorable thoughts and thought forms replacing the negative.

Concept of chakras, energy centers and dimensions

Remember ALL your choices affect everyone, all your chakras and 'ALL THAT IS'.

15 Chakras And Energy Centers - Table below created by author

# on Drawing	Location	Standard Chakra	John Ruskan	Kay C. Whitaker	Comment
1	Below the feet			Below the Feet	Moves a lot
2	Bottom of feet			Bottom of each foot	
3	Knees			Knees	
4	Base of spine	1-Root	1-Survival Center		
5	Between anus and vagina or testicles		2-Power Center		Controlling or giving power away
6	Hips			Hips	Smaller centers at hips move - sometimes outside the body
7	Below the Belly Button	2-Sacral	3- Sensation Center		Sensuality/Sexuality
8	Naval		4-Nurturing Center		
9	About one inch below the breast bone	3-Solar Plexus	5-Significance Center	Upper Belly	Smaller centers move. Psychological home of the ego
10	Center of Chest	4-Heart	6-Heart Center	Heart	
11	Throat, Mouth and Ears	5-Throat (Throat only)	7-Expression Center (Throat only)	Mouth, Ears and Throat	
12	Base of Skull in back		9-Creative Center		
13	Physical Eyes and Center of Forehead	6-Third Eye (center of forehead only)	8-Intuitive/Witness Center (center of forehead only)	Eyes	Can move a great deal. Sometimes expands itself into the center at the top of the head
14	Just outside the body, above the head	7-Crown	10-Spiritual Center	Just above the head	
15	Hands			Hands	Expand and shrink and move all around, even into other realms

15 Chakras And Energy Centers

I believe there are many more Chakras/Energy Centers than these fifteen; possibly an infinite number. These are the fifteen I work with. They are all affected by our choices.

Any more than these, I turn over to my Unihipili (subconscious), my super conscious and Spirit.

Use your own perception and awareness for any clarification and refinement.

The drawing below was created by the author

Notice that I used colors other than those normally associated with the seven most commonly known chakras. ALL chakras incorporate all colors. A specific color may be primary to a specific chakra.

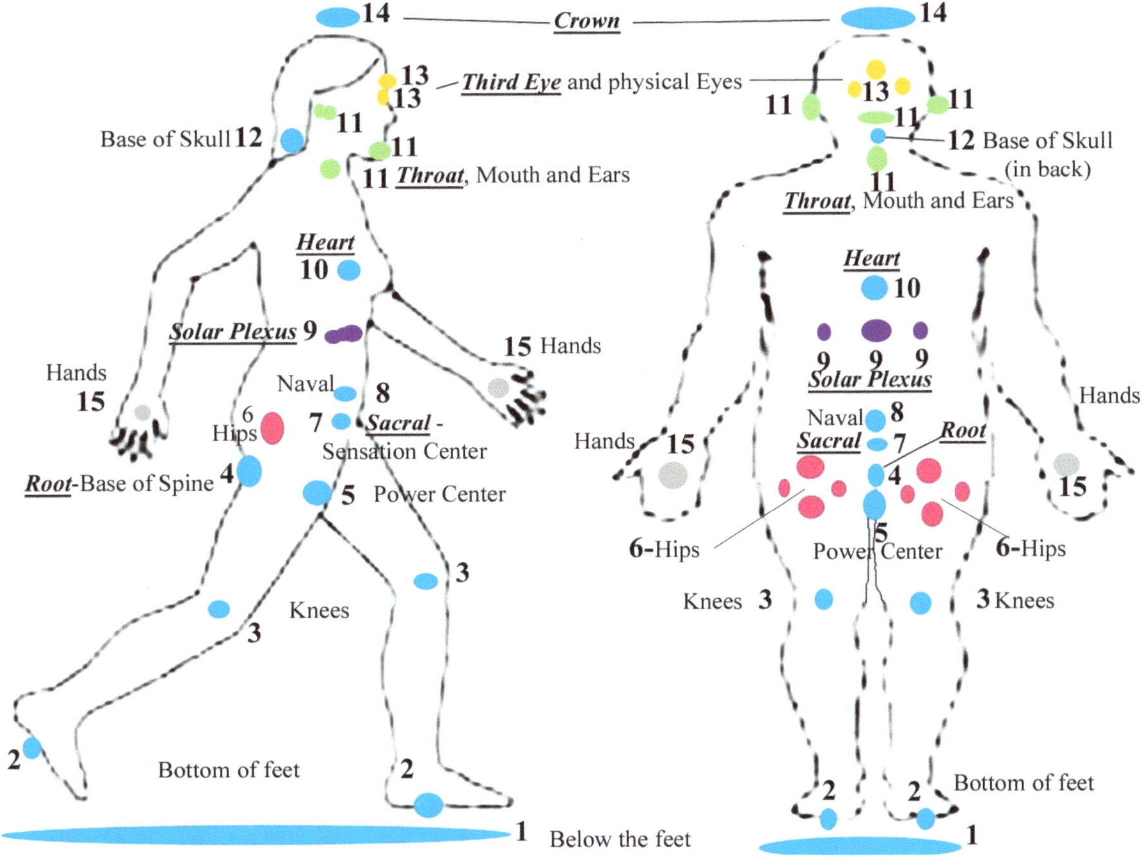

Graphic representation of

levels of consciousness

and an idea

of dimensions.

Graphic Representation is on the next page

This chart is one way to represent Consciousness levels and dimensions.

There are many different ways of thinking, different perceptions and different ways of representing concepts of 'Realities'. Any description is limiting. Please feel encouraged to develop your own map and then release it, except as a limited guide.

Universal Manifestation Templates are sometimes called 'Time Matrices'. There are uncountable Time Matrices within the Energy Matrix, which are often collectively referred as The Time Matrix.

All Time Matrices within the Cosmic Energy Matrix follow a specific mathematical-geometrical program through which space-time and matter can be experienced by consciousness.

Dimensions can be thought of as 'Platforms of Perception'.

Kristos: The word "Christos" (from which the word "Christian" later evolved) was originally spelled "Kristos" in the most ancient texts, and referred to the personal Divine Blueprint of Conscious Living God Energy of which all things and beings manifest are made.

DNA: Science does **not** yet recognize the true multi-strand DNA of human potential. The majority of the DNA strands corresponding to higher dimensional anatomy and consciousness have been largely dormant or damaged due to ancient blockages. The human body was designed to embody at least 12 dimensions of consciousness in one incarnation and has been corrupted. The original intention of Source was to remain fully conscious of Its connection to itself, regardless of how far It traveled into manifestation.

We are intimately connected with the earth. The body and the planet are built the same way - they both have an energetic grid.

The beings we call 'Guardians' are aspects of ourselves residing in what we often call higher dimensions.

Representation of levels of consciousness and an idea of dimensions

The table below was done by the author.

Divinity/Great Spirit/God/Source//All-That-Is						
The GOD SEED (I Am that I AM)						
MONADS According to some this is a direct aspect of the force you know of as God and is one aspect of God that makes you, your spirit, your higher-self, and your Soul uniquely you.						
Primary Thought and Sound Fields						
TM b						TM d
	Time Matrix C - The time Matrix (Universe and Parallel Universe) we are in				TM c - Parallel	
	H.U. 5	D-15	Universal - unmanifest	Anti Matter Universal Consciousness	PD-15	
		D-14	Consciousness - unmanifest		PD-14	
		D-13	Mind - unmanifest		PD-13	
	(Aveyon)	D-12	Nirvanic Mind - unmanifest	Avatar Identity. Able to ascend and descend through Dimensions 1 to 12 at will once skill is honed. Pre-Matter Liquid Light.	PD-12	
	H.U. 4	D-11	Buddhaic Mind - unmanifest		PD-11	
	(Vega)	D-10	Christaic Mind - unmanifest		PD-10	
	H.U. 3	D-9	Keriatic Mind - unmanifest	Over-Soul Identity Silica Based Life Form	PD-9	
		D-8	Monadic or Teura Mind		PD-8	
	(Gaia)	D-7	Ketheric Mind - Manifest		PD-7	
	H.U. 2	D-6	Angelic Mind - Manifest	Soul Identity Carbon Silica Based Life	PD-6	
		D-5	Archetype or Dora Mind - Manifest		PD-5	
	(Tara)	D-4	Astral Mind - Manifest		PD-4	
	(Earth)	D-3	Reasoning Mind, Mental Body - Manifest	Incarnate Identity Carbon Based	PD-3	
	H.U. 1	D-2	Instinctual or Emotional Mind - Manifest		PD-2	
		D-1	Unconscious Mind - Manifest		PD-1	

Personal Notes

Chapter 5

The Importance of the Subconscious and How to Strengthen Your Connection and Intuition

<u>There is nothing sub about the subconscious mind</u>.

The subconscious is more in touch with 'Reality' than the conscious mind.

It is vitally important to have a Loving, clear and cooperative relationship with your subconscious mind.

Thesaurus for 'sub': subordinate, secondary and junior, which are all adjectives.
This DOES **<u>NOT</u>** describe the subconscious mind.

Thesaurus for 'conscious': aware, awake, cognizant which are all adjectives.
The subconscious is more aware and awake than the conscious mind. Without the subconscious the conscious mind is pretty much asleep.

The super-conscious and conscious minds seem to be ok with being adjectives.

I prefer the Hawaiian name, Unihipili, for the subconscious mind. The Unihipili is more in touch with 'Reality' than the conscious mind. It may be lost and need guidance from the conscious mind to connect to LOVE, and once it is connected to LOVE it will help the conscious mind and all aspects of you connect more strongly to LOVE. If you consciously chose “Anything Else” the Unihipili will connect you to something other than LOVE.

I will be referring to the subconscious mind as Unihipili in most instances.

Willpower comes from the conscious mind. The cooperation of the Unihipili is needed for the choices to remain in effect.

The Unihipili (subconscious mind or child within) will respond or react according to your "choice." This child within is different than "the inner child" as used in inner child healing and soul retrieval. The inner child as used in ‘inner child work’ and soul retrieval **is a part of** the Unihipili.

As we increase the clarity and strength of communication between our conscious mind and the Unihipili, new energy, greater understanding, improved creativity and a knowingness of our life purpose will develop.

The Unihipili can also be thought of as the Gatekeeper. Some of our *feelings* and beliefs become our Gatekeeper. As you begin to become aware of and develop a LOVING relationship with the Unihipili (gatekeeper) your awareness of and access to the unknowable will also develop. Part of the Unihipili’s purpose is to protect us from becoming overwhelmed by accessing too much all at once.

The Unihipili is the link between the conscious mind and the super-conscious mind. Without this link/interpreter there is no connection, or a very weak and unconscious link.

Conceptual Graphic Of Unihipili

The graphic below was created by the author.

Unihipili as Gatekeeper:

> The Unihipili allows access to information from other dimensions/realities to the extent you are ready. It keeps you from being overwhelmed. Your conscious mind and conscious choices determine whether it connects to Divine LOVE or Anything Else.

Unihipili as Interpreter:

> The realm of Spirit normally does **not** speak your native language (for me it is English). We normally grasp the meaning as a rapid flow of thoughts, images, memories, feelings, concepts and awareness. There is often very little time to think about what you are receiving, and if you stop to think and analyze the flow usually stops. Save the analyzing and thinking until after the flow stops.

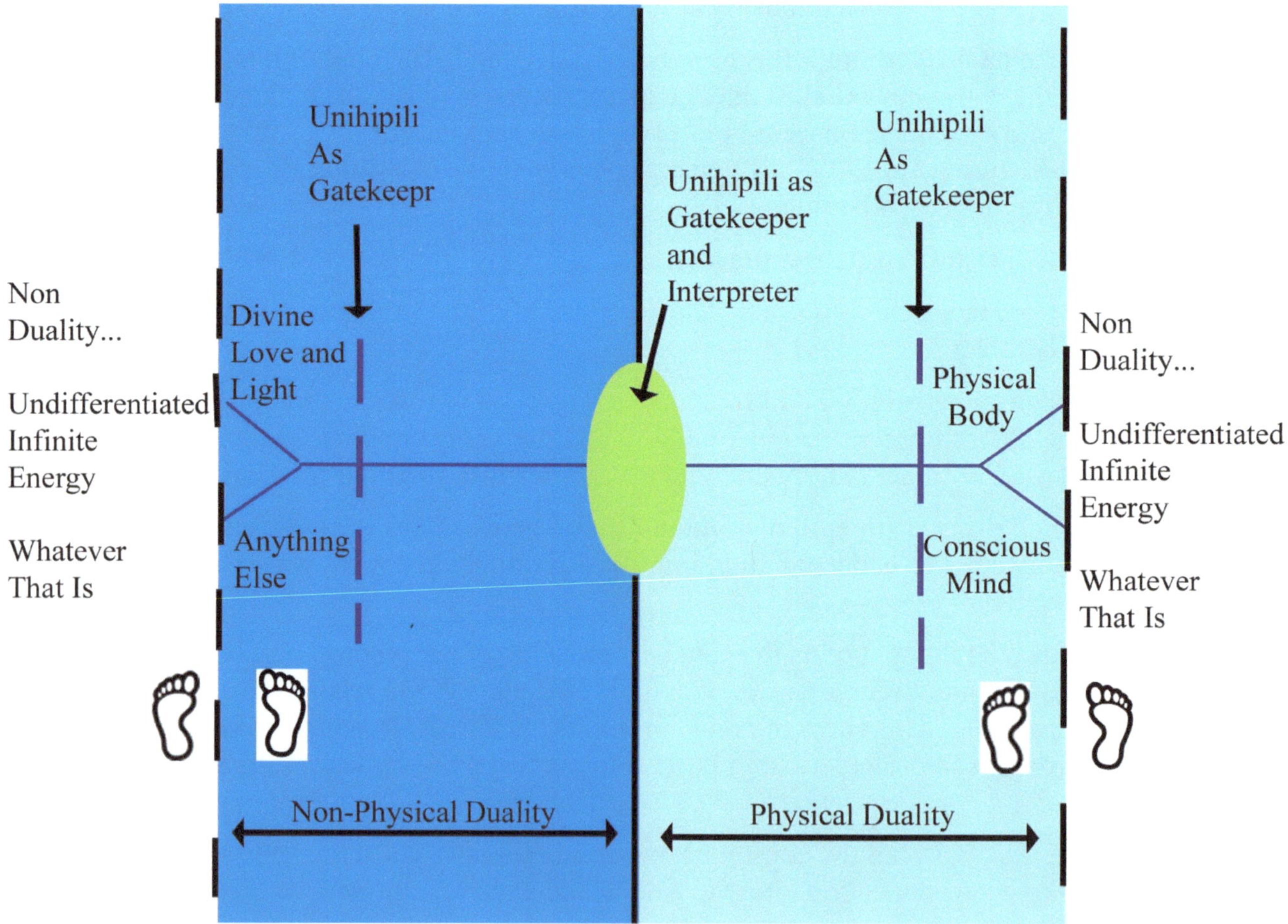

Another Conceptual Graphic Of Unihipili

The graphic below was created by the author.

I prefer the Hawaiian Name, Unihipili, for the subconscious mind

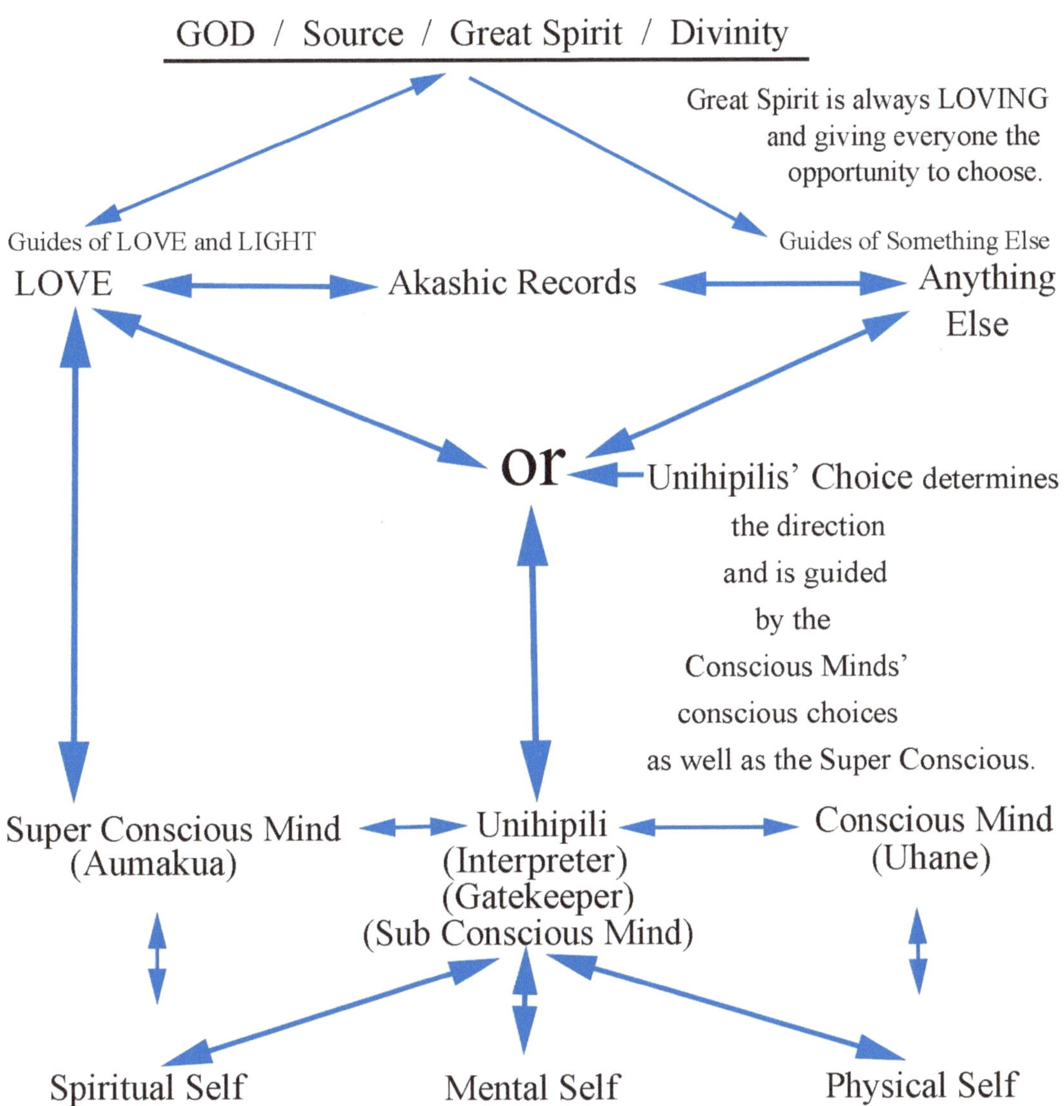

Willpower comes from the conscious mind. The cooperation of the Unihipili is needed for the choices to remain in effect.

Exercise To Connect To Your Unihipili With LOVE

To let the Unihipili know it is loved and to teach it and your conscious mind to communicate with each other and the Divine as is best, I suggest you do the following. This exercise will help you and your Unihipili's connection to become stronger and more loving.

Unihipili can be thought of as 'you' too. During the exercise the Unihipili will be referred to as *'U'*.

Exercise to consciously connect with your Unihipili:

From a state of LOVE, say hello to your Unihipili. "Hello, I love you and am happy that we are strengthening our bond. Please show me a representation of what you look like and/or give me a sense of you. *Thank you.*

You may get a vision and/or *feeling* of a very small child who is sad, lost, lonely and/or angry. Then again, you may find a happy child who is already fairly mature, connected, happy and LOVING.

Ask permission before continuing to strengthen the bond with LOVE using steps 1-4 below:

1) Hold your hands out in front of you, at shoulder level, with the palms up, in invitation. Allow the Unihipili to approach. When you see or sense that *'U'* is present and ready, position your hands, palms down, on Unihipili's shoulders with LOVE.
When it *feels* right, ask Unihipili, "Are we ready for the next exercise?"

2) Again hold your hands out in front of you, at shoulder level, with your palms down. Allow the Unihipili to approach you and stand up so your hands are touching the top of *'U's"* head. Gently stroke the top of *'U's"* head or just allow *'U'* to stand there and experience your LOVE.
When it *feels* right, ask Unihipili, "Are we ready for the next exercise?"

3) Now hold your arms out wide, with your palms facing in, and allow Unihipili to approach you. Allow *'U'* to hug you, and only when invited, slowly, gently and lovingly close your arms for a mutual hug. Allow Unihipili to experience your LOVE.
When it *feels* right, ask Unihipili, "Are we ready for the next exercise?"

4) Finally, hold your hands out in front of you at waist level with your palms up. Allow the Unihipili to approach you and put *'U's"* hand on yours. You may stroke each other's hands to share the LOVE.
When it *feels* right, tell Unihipili, "I love you and thank you". Be open to any response and when done open your eyes.

Only with reverence, LOVE, and self-discipline will you win your Unihipili's cooperation. When allowed, Unihipili will respond automatically and you will have a renewed and powerful helper.

Remember to maintain communication with your Unihipili and to support Unihipili, realizing that even though it is very powerful, *'U'* is in many ways childlike and innocent.

Preferably every morning and evening, or at least when prompted, request the following:

1) "Unihipili, please always remember to stay connected to and accept things from Great Spirit and Great Spirit's Helpers of Pure Divine LOVE and LIGHT only."

2) "Is there anything you want or need: toys, nourishment, clothes, swim/bath/shower, laundry bag, backpack, laundry done or guidance by me or Great Spirit"? Allow the Unihipili to choose as long as what *'U'* chooses is of Pure Divine LOVE and LIGHT.

Remember the Unihipili is present in a non-physical realm, so *'U'* is free from the rules of the physical world. The Unihipili can wear anything *'U'* wants; eat as much as *'U'* wants; have *'U's"* backpack as large or as small as *'U'* wants, and any color. The backpack and its contents are also free from the rules of the physical world and can be expanded or contracted as the Unihipili desires, therefore the Unihipili can carry as much as *'U'* wants by shrinking and then re-expanding the items. Allow *"U"* to play!

Personal Notes

Chapter 6
Contemplation, Meditation and Prayer
The Basics

Always make absolutely sure that you are connected to God Source/Great Spirit when contemplating, meditating and praying. I suggest a prayer as follows: "Great Spirit and Great Spirit Helpers of Pure Divine LOVE and LIGHT keep me connected to You and only to You. *Thank You.*

Contemplation:
Have a thought or question to reflect on at the conscious level.

An example would be: "Is it best if I move to California?"

Some begin meditation by contemplating their breath. After focusing on the breath they then either meditate ***or*** contemplate on a challenge/problem/solution/question.

Meditation:
After contemplation, let go of all conscious thoughts to the best of your ability.
With practice you will be in a silent place with a direct connection to Great Spirit and Guides of Divine LOVE and LIGHT. You may still hear an airplane, people talking, or some other outside noise. You may have thoughts flow into your conscious mind. Let them flow through without trying to block them or latching onto them. Some are totally unaware of all outside influences and yet they will become instantly alert and come back into what most perceive as a conscious state if there is an immediate need. Allow your conscious mind to rest and allow your subconscious mind and super conscious mind to explore **without thought. Be the observer.**

Flow:
Flow is beyond contemplation or meditation. It is like a continuous two way communication with what is beyond the conscious minds' ability to fully analyze or understand. We need the Unihipili (subconscious mind) to interpret the flow for us. Unconditional surrender to Great Spirit/Divinity is the key to flow, bringing in an authentic and continual state of flow to and from Divinity. Controlling nothing you control everything. Only by taking control can you lose control.

Prayer:
Prayer is basically a sincere attempt to communicate with Source and the Divine within yourself. The key is to be present, authentic and sincere with LOVE in your heart. Practice your own prayers instead of repeating others' words from memory. Too often prayer is a last resort and we are turning to prayer in desperation. Prayer is often only practiced when we want something. A prayer of gratitude and thanks is much more beneficial.

Another way to think of this:

Contemplation is asking your God-self about something and being open to answers.

Meditation is opening yourself and **listening** to your God-self without conscious thought.

Flow is allowing an unrestricted communication with God while going about your daily life.

Prayer is a sincere attempt to **communicate with or to** God Source and the Divine within yourself.

Personal Notes

Chapter 7

Clearing and Healing
(Past, present and future combined in this single moment)

Prayer

Prayer is basically a sincere attempt to communicate with and to Source and the Divine within yourself. The key is to be present, authentic and sincere with LOVE in your heart. Practice your own prayers instead of repeating others' from memory.

Affirmations

Affirmations are often described as positive statements. They are used to retrain the Unihipili (subconscious mind) and create constructive changes in yourself and the physical world.

Every thought and word is an affirmation. All of our inner dialogues are streams of affirmations. Saying and thinking positive affirmations will help to shift you from the negative to the positive. Each negative thought and word will create more of the negative. Affirmations work on the level of the Unihipili (subconscious mind) and are very powerful. Avoiding the use of the words *not, but, need to, try, want to, should* and *could* is critical in affirmations. Realize *don't, won't, can't* and *shouldn't* are all "*not*" words.

The Universe only understands "yes". It is critical to use the positive counterpart of any negative. If you find yourself thinking or saying something negative or unkind say to yourself and the universe, "cancel/clear", and rethink or reword with something positive and kind.

If you say, "I will not be Angry" or "I am not angry", the Universe hears, "I will be angry" or "I am angry".

Instead say, "I will be forgiving, LOVING" or "I am forgiving, LOVING" (unconditional love).

If you have difficulty thinking of an appropriate word, use the positive word or words that come the closest.

Interestingly, when you think or say, "I am not happy", the universe keeps the 'not' in place and energizes the opposite of happy. Be mindful of how you think and speak.

If there are negative and/or limiting feelings, emotions, memories or beliefs involved, the effectiveness of positive affirmations <u>may</u> be limited until the feelings, emotions, memories replaying or beliefs involved are cleared and healed. Sometimes the affirmation itself creates the clearing.

At first, it may be difficult for you to avoid using the thoughts or words *not, try, need to, should*. It gets easier with practice. In normal daily conversation and occasionally when doing healing I still catch myself using negative or limiting words. Thinking positive thoughts, saying positive words and re-wording your thoughts and statements will become easier with practice and forgiveness.

The best explanations and example I have found are by Louise L. Hay in the book '*You Can Heal Your Life*'. (http://www.louisehay.com/)

Memories Replaying

Memories replaying like old tapes, from past experiences, keep negative and limiting beliefs energized.

For example, one might delete an email, however, until the 'deleted' folder is emptied and the email is permanently trashed the email is still there and so is the message.

Self I-dentity Ho'oponopono: The best explanations and example I have found are by Ihaleakala Hew Len in the book *'Zero Limits'.* I have been unable to find a web site that is Ihaleakala Hew Lens'. His teachings are very powerful, however many people have commercialized them. Two Web Sites you might find of interest.

(http://zero-wise.com/ihhl and http://www.drcat.org/articles_interviews/html/hotfudge.html)

Trapped Feelings/Emotions and Inherited Trapped Feelings/Emotions

One of the two ways I have found the simplest and most effective way to clear and release trapped or suppressed feelings/emotions is explained in detail in the book, "*The Emotion Code*", by Dr. Bradley Nelson

(http://www.drbradleynelson.com).

Suppressed and Repressed Feelings/Emotions

The second way I have found to be one of the simplest and most effective ways to clear and release trapped, suppressed or repressed feelings/emotions is explained in detail in the book, "*EMOTIONAL CLEARING: An East/West Guide to Releasing Negative Feelings and Awakening Unconditional Happiness'* by John Ruskan(http://www.emclear.com/index.html).

Whether you choose a method to clear feelings and emotions based on Bradley Nelson, John Ruskan or someone else, clear *both trapped and suppressed/repressed* feelings and emotions. Also, as you pursue clearing you will become able to clear feelings and emotions when it is best to wait. Bradley Nelson asks "Do I have a trapped emotion I can release now?" I suggest you ask, "Do I have a trapped or suppressed feeling or emotion it is best I release now?"

Unresolved Feelings/Emotions

Feelings and Emotions that are unresolved can be cleared and released using the same methods as above. These are feelings and emotions that you are aware of to some extent at the conscious level.

Negative and Limiting Beliefs

Negative and limiting/interfering beliefs are always caused by and energized by trapped, suppressed, repressed, unresolved feelings and emotions and/or by memories replaying. Even if a belief is cleared, it may be re-energized unless the underlying feeling, emotion or memory replaying has been healed, transmuted, released and integrated. The belief is often cleared by clearing and healing the feelings, emotions and memories replaying that energized it. If the negative/limiting belief remains after the feelings, emotions and memories replaying have been cleared, the belief itself can be cleared using the same methods as listed below.

Some ways to heal, transmute, release and integrate the underlying feeling, emotion or memory replaying are;

1) Prayer (It is sometimes as simple as a quick prayer)
2) Affirmations (unless there is a limiting belief interfering)
3) Healing and releasing 'Memories Replaying' based on Self Identity Ho'oponopono
4) Healing and releasing trapped feelings and emotions based on Bradley Nelson's *"Emotion Code"*, and
5) Healing and releasing feelings and emotions based on John Ruskan's *"Emotional Clearing."*

Additionally, keep thoughts about the future positive and without attachment to any specific outcome. Allow your Higher Self and Great Spirit to guide you moment by moment.

Personal Notes

Chapter 8

Main Tool - Great Spirit Prayers

Prayer Basics

1) It's ok to use the word 'God' or any name you are comfortable with, so long as you remember any attempt on our part to describe or define God is limiting. My personal preference is to use 'Great Spirit'.
2) I prefer the Hawaiian names for the levels of mind as follows:
   a) **Aumakua** (Spirit, Super Conscious Mind, Over Soul, Higher Self) compares every new experience and thought with Truth - The Universal Law Itself.
   b) **Unihipili** (Soul Mind, Pre-Conscious Mind, Subconscious Mind) compares every new experience and thought with every related experience and thought you have had in all your lifetimes.
   c) **Uhane** (Conscious Mind) compares each new experience and each new thought with all the experiences and thoughts of a related nature that you have had in this present lifetime.
      (As thoughts come to the Uhane, they may be very subtle. You then have a choice to dismiss them; heal, transmute, release and integrate them as is best; or bring them further into your consciousness and investigate them.)

I recommend that you say the 'Prayer Underlay' on the following page before saying any of the other prayers and that you say the prayers on the two pages headed 'Every Morning and Evening' often. Say the rest of the prayers as often as you are prompted.

I also recommend you do the 'Daily Check' at the beginning of Chapter 9 at least once each day.

Some Further Explanations and Re-iteration

1) Please: The word 'please' is avoided in these prayers. Too many people use the word please without faith and in supplication in a way that gives power away. These prayers are to a Power that is within, without and everywhere. They are requests, commands, and petitions to the Higher Aspects of your God-self.

2) Help: The word 'help', as used in these prayers, is a request for assistance and aid rather than a plea for some outside force to do the work.

3) Keep it so and (Make it so):
Is a request to a Power that is within, without and everywhere. They are requests, commands, and petitions to the Higher Aspects of your God-self.

4) Violet Flame: Some have asked or wondered what the Violet Flame' is. Several definitions combined into one is that, 'The Violet Flame' is the essence of a unique Spiritual Light which has the qualities of mercy, forgiveness, freedom and transmutation". Trust that it is of GOD SOURCE.

Prayer Underlay To Make Other Prayers More Effective

I suggest you say this prayer underlay at least once before saying the prayers on the rest of the pages. You may want to say the prayer underlay occasionally to make the rest of the prayers even more effective.

Great Spirit and Great Spirit Helpers, as are best,
Keep it so my 'Heart Prayer', Mind Prayer' and 'Word Prayer' are always completely in tune with each other and Your LOVE. *Thank You.*

The following three prayers may seem redundant. This is done purposely for the Unihipili.

1) Great Spirit and Great Spirit Helpers, as are best,
   Keep it so "I", "my", "me", or "myself" refer to all aspects of myself, including my Aumakua, my Unihipili, my Uhane, (Full Birth Name), all past, present and future selves, my Spirit Guides, soul pieces, and the primary parallel selves for each in all dimensions, realities, time frames and in 'All That Is'. *Thank You.*
2) Great Spirit and Great Spirit Helpers, as are best,
   When I pray for others, keep it so all aspects of them, including their Aumakua, their Unihipili, their Uhane, their incarnate human self, all their past, present and future selves, their Spirit Guides, their soul pieces, and the primary parallel selves for each in all dimensions, realities, time frames and in 'All That Is' are included as is best. *Thank You.*
3) Great Spirit and Great Spirit Helpers, as are best,
   Keep it so all prayers apply to us in all times, past, present and future, in all dimensions and in all realities. Keep it so all prayers apply to the Feminine/Female, the Masculine/Male, the actual physical DNA, the cellular and muscular memory, and the physical and non-physical selves' minds and bodies. Keep it so all clearings and healings are in alignment with and attuned to Your Pure Divine LOVE and according to the 'Divine Plan' (Original Blueprint) and 'Divine Manifestation'(The Original Weaving). *Thank You.*

Great Spirit and Great Spirit Helpers, as are best,
Keep it so all prayers include all aspects of myself and others as is best. *Thank You.*

Great Spirit and Great Spirit Helpers, as are best,
Keep it so I Know and am aware that all persons and Beings, including what are typically thought of as inanimate and manmade, are actually aspects of myself. *Thank You.*

Great Spirit and Great Spirit Helpers, as are best,
Help me to remain truly humble, discerning, vigilant, diligent, unconditionally accepting, and Loving through all these prayers and as Our healing is done. *Thank You.*

Great Spirit and Great Spirit Helpers, as are best,
Always include a Helper of pure Divine LOVE and LIGHT, as is best, who Knows and understands Earth time and space and human needs and desires. *Thank You.*

Great Spirit and Great Spirit Helpers, as are best,
Keep it so my needs and desires are in harmony with and attuned to YOUR LOVE and LIGHT and 'The Divine Manifestation'. *Thank You.*

Great Spirit and Great Spirit Helpers, as are best,
Include the above in all prayers, requests, declarations, clearings, healings and affirmations as is best. *Thank You.*

Every Morning and Evening

Great Spirit and Great Spirit Helpers, as are best,
Keep it so my 'Heart Prayer', 'Mind Prayer' and 'Word Prayer' are always completely in tune with each other and Your LOVE. *Thank You.*

Great Spirit and Great Spirit Helpers, as are best,
Help me to Know when to speak, when to share and when to be silent. Help me to recognize and follow Your guidance, always sharing as is best. *Thank You.*

Great Spirit and Great Spirit Helpers, as are best,
Help me stay fully connected to YOU and YOUR LOVE and LIGHT. *Thank You.*

Great Spirit and Great Spirit Helpers, as are best,
Help me stay standing fully in YOUR LOVE, LIGHT and VIOLET FLAME. *Thank You.*

Great Spirit and Great Spirit Helpers, as are best,
Keep me completely surrounded by YOUR LOVE, LIGHT and VIOLET FLAME. *Thank You.*

Great Spirit and Great Spirit Helpers, as are best,
Help me stay filled with Your LOVE, LIGHT and VIOLET FLAME as is best. *Thank You.*

Great Spirit and Great Spirit Helpers, as are best,
Help me keep it so only energies and beings of Pure Divine LOVE and LIGHT surround me, influence me and share and communicate through me. *Thank You.*

Great Spirit and Great Spirit Helpers, as are best,
Help me to always keep Your Sacred Space of LOVE open for me as is best and help me to always stay in Our Sacred Space. *Thank You.*

Great Spirit and Great Spirit Helpers, as are best,
Help me to keep my thoughts, my heart, my feelings and my soul Positive, Loving, Pure and Radiant. *Thank You.*

Great Spirit and Great Spirit Helpers, as are best,
Surround and fill all my family, pets, friends, acquaintances, relatives, and relations with Your LOVE, LIGHT and VIOLET FLAME as is best. Walk with them and help them as is best. *Thank You.*

Great Spirit and Great Spirit Helpers, as are best,
Help me to surround and fill my home, vehicle, place of business and everything in and around them with Your LOVE, LIGHT and VIOLET FLAME as is best. Walk with us and help us as is best. Do the same with all I come in contact with and communicate with. *Thank You.*

Great Spirit and Great Spirit Helpers, as are best,
Help me remain constantly aware of all entities, energies and influences as is best. *Thank You.*

Great Spirit and Great Spirit Helpers, as are best,
Help me to always see, hear, sense, feel and be aware, as is best. Include all physical and non-physical paths of information as is best. Help me recognize and understand the messages and guidance. *Thank You.*

Every Morning and Evening continued

Great Spirit and Great Spirit Helpers, as are best,
Help me to always fill all voids and emptiness with 100% Pure Divine LOVE and LIGHT as is best. *Thank You.*

Great Spirit and Great Spirit Helpers, as are best,
Help me remember I am Divine LOVE and that I am ONE with YOU. *Thank You.*

Great Spirit and Great Spirit Helpers, as are best,
Help me to always keep all aspects of myself in harmony, alignment and attunement, so we share and heal in union with each other and with Your Pure Divine LOVE. Help me to Know and have Faith that You will do as is best with every situation in Your Pure Divine LOVE. *Thank You.*

Great Spirit and Great Spirit Helpers, as are best,
Help me to always make choices and decisions that are for Great Spirits' LOVE and that are in harmony with and attuned to my highest good and physical well-being and the highest good and well-being of all. *Thank You.*

Great Spirit and Great Spirit Helpers, as are best,
Help me to choose, to have chosen and to be in the 'Law of Grace' and do what is best for the Highest good of All. *Thank You.*

Great Spirit and Great Spirit Helpers, as are best,
Help me to maintain my determination, perseverance and Faith at all times. *Thank You.*

Great Spirit and Great Spirit Helpers, as are best,
Help me to let go of and release ALL attachments and just 'Be'. *Thank You.*

Great Spirit and Great Spirit Helpers, as are best,
Help me stay grounded and fully connected to EARTH and all of Her Selves through CENTRAL SUN and YOUR LOVE and help me keep EARTH and all Her Selves connected to CENTRAL SUN through me, so we heal each other with and through YOUR LOVE and LIGHT. *Thank You.*

Great Spirit and Great Spirit Helpers, as are best,
Help me receive from only You and Your Divine LOVE and LIGHT, all answers, knowingness, awareness, intuition and guidance. Help me to understand these as best. *Thank You.*

Humility and Diligence

Great Spirit and Great Spirit Helpers, as are best,
Help me remain truly humble, discerning, vigilant, diligent, unconditionally accepting, determined and LOVING as Our healing and sharing is done. *Thank You.*

Clearing, Filling and Surrounding Yourself With Divine LOVE and LIGHT

Any time during the day, this prayer can be said when something needs to be healed, cleared and released.

Great Spirit and Great Spirit Helpers, as are best,

1) Help me to always live within Pure Divine LOVE and LIGHT and guide me to always embody my highest purpose and highest good. *Thank You.*
2) Help me to use the VIOLET FLAME and all other methods as are best to fully see, heal, transmute, release, integrate, balance, align and attune all situations and all energies as is best. *Thank You.* (be specific during the day when it *feels* 'right')
3) Help me to see, heal, transmute, release and integrate as is best, all that had been blocking or limiting me. *Thank You.*
   (Remember to do your part by prayer, positive affirmations, de-energizing memories replaying and by releasing trapped or suppressed feelings/emotions).
4) Help me do what is best with the energies involved. *Thank You.*
5) Help me acknowledge, activate and integrate all positive aspects that have been hidden, forgotten and/or suppressed. *Thank You.*
6) Help me to fill all voids and emptiness with 100% Pure Divine LOVE and LIGHT as is best. *Thank You.*
7) Help me do the same, as is best, for all places, persons, beings and everything I have or will come in contact with and/or have communication with. *Thank You.*

Great Spirit and Great Spirit Helpers, as are best,
Help me to stay connected to only You and Your PURE LOVE and LIGHT. *Thank You.*

Great Spirit and Great Spirit Helpers, as are best,
Help me to always fully stand in Your LOVE and LIGHT and in THE VIOLET FLAME. *Thank You.*

Great Spirit and Great Spirit Helpers, as are best,
Help me receive from only You and Your Divine LOVE and LIGHT, all answers, knowingness, awareness, intuition and guidance. Help me to understand these as best. *Thank You.*

Wisdom and Peace

Great Spirit and Great Spirit Helpers, as are best,
Help me to continue to develop the resources, Knowingness, Awareness and the Wisdom so that I conduct my life in Peace and LOVE. As my Awareness and Wisdom expand, help me to Know and understand all that it is time for me to Know moment by moment. *Thank You.*

Great Spirit and Great Spirit Helpers, as are best,
Help me to always remain Neutral and Centered in myself. *Thank You.*
Help me to always walk in Balance and to Practice Divine LOVE. *Thank You.*
Help me to always choose Harmony, Peace and LOVE. *Thank You.*
Help me to always recognize Your Guidance and to understand it as is best. *Thank You.*
Help me to always be my True Self and follow my Truth and my Path as guided by YOU. *Thank You.*
Help me to always allow others their own Truths. *Thank You.*
Help me to always allow others their own Paths. *Thank You.*
Help me to always LOVE myself and all others unconditionally. *Thank You.*
Help me to always heal, align and attune with LOVE. *Thank You.*
Help me to always LOVE and embrace ALL THAT I AM unconditionally. *Thank You.*
Help me to always listen to the promptings of Great Spirit. *Thank You.*
Help me to always release all anxiety and impatience and to heal the underlying causes. *Thank You.*
Help me to always be totally honest with myself. *Thank You.*

Help me to heal, transmute, release and integrate all superstitions, dogma, negative/limiting feelings, emotions, beliefs and memories replaying. *Thank You.*

Help me to heal the ego by releasing, with LOVE, all negative/limiting feelings, emotions, memories replaying, beliefs and fears that no longer serve my highest good.. *Thank You.*

Help me to Know my life's purposes and to always persevere with total Faith and unconditional acceptance. *Thank You.*

Help me to always be in a state of Beingness that simply allows. *Thank You.*
Help me to always choose Great Spirit and LOVE. *Thank You.*

Great Spirit and Great Spirit Helpers, as are best,
Share, speak and communicate through me, as is best. *Thank You.*

Help me to keep it so only You and Your Divine LOVE can share and communicate through me. *Thank You.*

Great Spirit and Great Spirit Helpers, as are best,
Help me to Know when to speak, when to share and when to be silent, always sharing as is best. *Thank You.*

Great Spirit and Great Spirit Helpers, as are best,
Help me to always acknowledge and to be grateful for Your LOVE and Your Guidance. Help me keep it so LOVE flows through all I AM and attunes me with You. I give thanks for the contribution that I make to the Whole. *Thank You.*

Manifesting and Moving Forward

Great Spirit and Great Spirit Helpers, as are best,
Assist me in seeing, healing, transmuting, releasing and integrating as is best, in Pure Divine LOVE, all that had been blocking or limiting me (memories replaying, feelings/emotions, thoughts and beliefs). Help me to keep it so my desires, intentions, co-creations and manifestations are for my highest good, well-being within duality and for the highest good and well-being of all. *Thank You*

Great Spirit and Great Spirit Helpers, as are best,
Help me to keep it so that all my desires, intentions, and manifestations are in Harmony and alignment with Your Pure Divine LOVE. Help me to stay attuned to Your Pure Divine LOVE, LIGHT, greater joy, happiness, peace, ease, prosperity, abundance and fun. *Thank You.*

Great Spirit and Great Spirit Helpers, as are best,

1) Help me so my 'Heart Prayer', 'Mind Prayer' and 'Word Prayer' are always completely in harmony and attunement with each other and Your LOVE. *Thank You.*
2) Help me to always draw strength, wisdom, support and potential through You. *Thank You.*
3) Help me so I always remain fully connected with You. *Thank You.*
4) Help me to have total Faith and Trust in You. *Thank You.*
5) Help me to have completely accepted Your LOVE and Grace with thanks and gratitude. *Thank You.*
6) Help me to have totally healed, transmuted, released and integrated, as is best, all that had been blocking or limiting me. *Thank You.*
7) Help me to have fully surrendered to You and Your LOVE in order to bring all Your bounty into this world and incorporate this bounty into me and my 'reality'. *Thank You.*
8) Help me so that with each step our creative potential, in tune with LOVE, blesses, co-creates and manifests 'All That Is'. *Thank You.*
9) Help me to know and be fully aware that co-creation and manifestation begins with subconscious and conscious thoughts and choices. To co-create or manifest something here on earth the thought and choice comes first.

    Sometimes the action is as simple as: have a thought and then say something or make an assessment based on the thought.

    Other times the action is more obvious, such as when you get a new car . You first have the thought of a new car, then decide what kind of car you want, then figure out the finances, then go shopping, then pay for it.

    For a garden you first have the thought of a garden. You then decide where, how big, what supplies you need and what you want to plant. You finally get the supplies and seeds or small plants, dig or build a raised bed, and plant. You will probably need to water the plants and maybe give them some shade.

    For a job or source of income the process is the same. Thought followed by actions.

10) Help me to always have thoughts that are in full harmony and alignment with Pure Divine LOVE and help me to finish the manifestation by taking action too, as is best. *Thank You.*

Graphic Representation to show a person standing in, filled with and surrounded by Divine LOVE, LIGHT and VIOLET FLAME

Graphic Representation on next page

The large Cone of Divinity represents the evolution of a consciousness from lower to higher energy levels or vibrational frequencies. The color white represents Divine LOVE and LIGHT, the wide outline represents the Divine VIOLET FLAME. The face represents the 'I AM' presence within a person/being and one's Spirit Guardians.

Note that the bottom of the Cone of Divinity is too narrow to fully contain an individual's whole self. This leaves the individual open to influence from other persons/beings, even those that are uncomfortable existing in a state of LOVE. Also note the presence of a barrier right at the point that the Cone of Divinity becomes wide enough to accommodate a person/being. This barrier serves to protect those who are just starting to 'wake up' from powerful unwholesome influences. This barrier seems to be permeable, however it does help to protect those who are still developing their connection to Divinity and/or their protection.

Upon passing through the barrier, the person/being loses the protection it affords and needs to learn how to protect their self. The barrier also serves to keep them from descending to levels below it and thus regaining its protective value. At this point it is critically important to stay within the Cone of Divinity by remaining in a state of Divine LOVE at all times. If the person/being leaves the state of Divine LOVE for whatever reason, they are open to unwholesome influences, unless they have surrounded themselves with Divine LOVE, LIGHT and VIOLET FLAME. The technique of filling and surrounding one's self with Divine LOVE, LIGHT and VIOLET FLAME is a critical skill to master, especially when the Divine Plan calls for you to interact with entities who have yet to choose Divine LOVE and LIGHT.

Upon further growth, you will rise above perceived negativity, and the width of the Cone of Divinity begins to encompass everything. At this point, the consciousness itself has become so LOVING that unwholesome influences find you distasteful and begin to avoid you.

It is important to note that while one is only partially within The Cone of Divinity at its narrow bottom, it is possible and beneficial to simply be in contact. This can be accomplished by simply asking for help from the 'Universe', in the name of Divinity.

Beings progress from unconscious to higher levels of consciousness at different rates. Do your best and let go of any impatience.

We are all headed to the same place. As you practice forgiveness and LOVE and your essences LIGHT rises you will notice resistance and what you may perceive as attacks from yourself and the Shadow Collective. As you reach the higher frequencies notice that you need to travel through layers of darkness. The layer of darkness just below "The Light" is the most powerful. Ask Great Spirit to keep you standing in Great Spirits Pure Love and Light. Ask Great Spirit and Great Spirits Helpers of Pure Divine Love and Light to fill you and surround you with Pure Love, Light and Violet Flame. Also notice that the distance for your communication with the Light becomes shorter and the pathway wider and clearer as your consciousness rises.

Graphic Representation to show a person standing in, filled with and surrounded by Divine LOVE, LIGHT and VIOLET FLAME

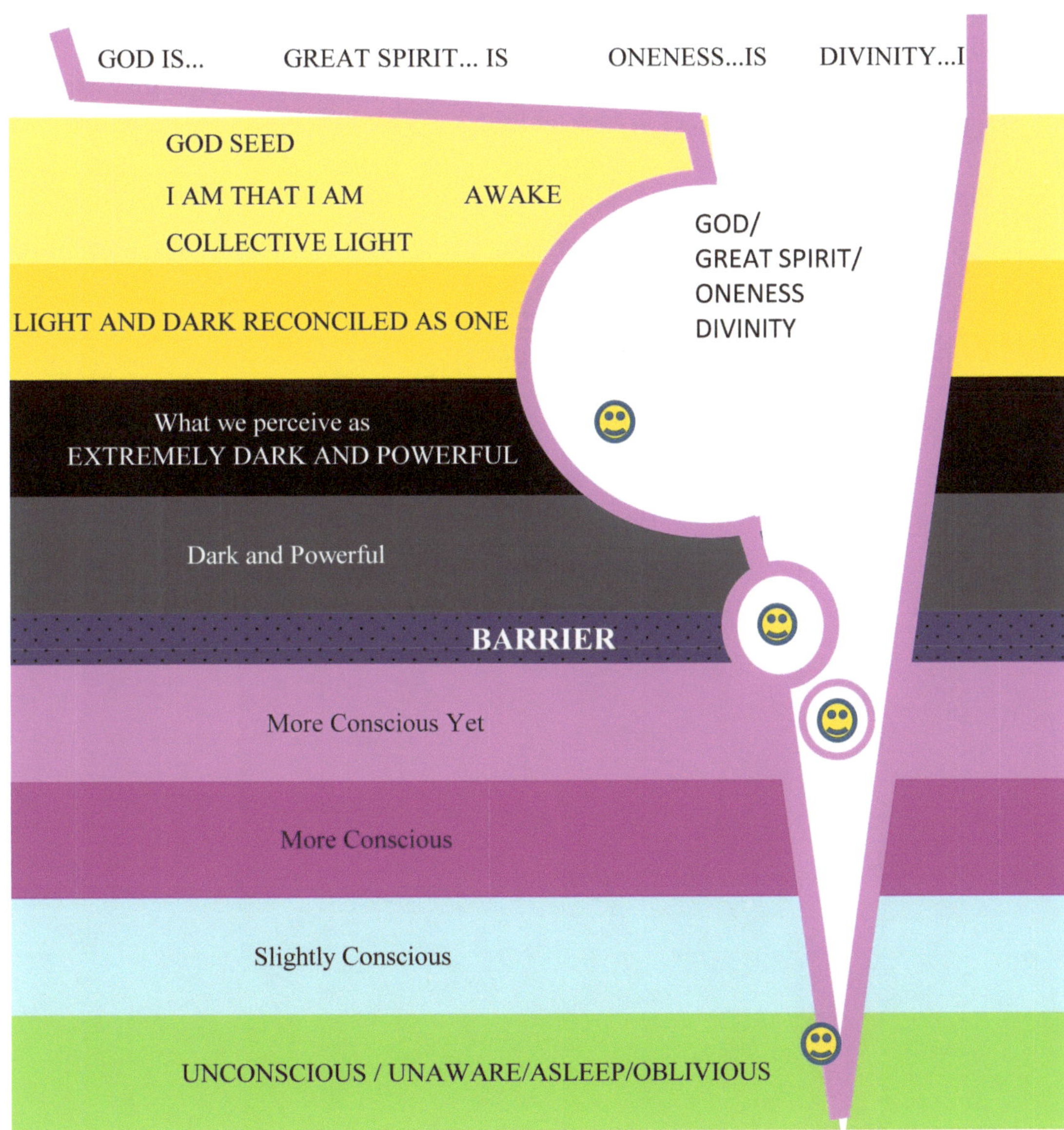

Gratitude

Great Spirit and Great Spirit Helpers,
Thank you for the Earth.
Thank you for the Water.
Thank you for the Air.
Thank you for the Fire.
Thank you for the LOVE and the LIGHT.

My Relations

Great Spirit and Great Spirit Helpers, as are best,
Surround and fill all my family, pets, friends, acquaintances, relatives, and relations with Your LOVE, LIGHT and VIOLET FLAME as is best and walk with them as is best. Help them and protect them as is best. *Thank You.*

Great Spirit and Great Spirit Helpers, as are best,
Help me to always be grateful for the life of all my relations and all creation, both corporal and non-corporal. *(The birds, animals, fish, insects, reptiles, trees, grass, plants, shrubs, dirt, rocks, minerals, mountains, plains, valleys, streams, rivers, lakes, oceans, clouds, rain, thunder, lightening, air, fire, sky, sun, stars, moon, planets, galaxies, universes, all galactic beings.) Thank You.*

Chapter 9
Other Tools
Tool 2 - Daily Check

This page is a daily check you can do to make sure you are connected to Great Spirit and Great Spirit's Helpers of Pure Divine LOVE and LIGHT only, and are getting everything from Great Spirit's LOVE and LIGHT. You may want to do the 'check' several times per day if you feel it is best. Use your own way of getting answers. Some ways of checking are by the use of a pendulum, muscle testing (kinesiology), a physical sensation, a visual sign or a knowingness/Awareness.
If you are new to this type of testing, you may want to say a few prayers. (see end of this tool for an example)

To begin, check to make sure you are getting 'yes', 'no', 'inappropriate to ask' and 'unable to answer' clearly

Great Spirit, show me "yes".
Great Spirit, show me "no".
Great Spirit, show me "inappropriate to ask."
Great Spirit, show me "unable to answer".

If you get a 'no' on any of the following questions, you have something to clear.

Great Spirit, I am connected to you and your helpers of pure Divine LOVE, LIGHT and VIOLET FLAME only.
Great Spirit, I am standing fully in your LOVE, LIGHT and VIOLET FLAME.
Great Spirit, I am completely filled by your LOVE, LIGHT and VIOLET FLAME as is best.
Great Spirit, I am completely and fully surrounded by your LOVE, LIGHT and VIOLET FLAME.
Great Spirit, I am clear, as is best.
Great Spirit, I am clear about myself, as is best.
Great Spirit, I am clear about (___my full birth name___), as is best.
Great Spirit, I am clear about (___use any other name(s) you go by, one at a time___), as is best.
Great Spirit, I am clear about all others, as is best.
Great Spirit, I am fully attuned to you, as is best.
(optional) Great Spirit, I am clear about (___fill in the blank___), as is best. Use this for someone or something specific if you are in doubt.

To end, double check as follows.
Great Spirit, show me "yes".
Great Spirit, show me "no".
Great Spirit, show me "inappropriate to ask."
Great Spirit, show me "unable to answer".
Great Spirit, you and your helpers of pure Divine LOVE and LIGHT have answered all my/our questions.

To clear and heal the above:
Great Spirit and Great Spirit Helpers, as are best,
Make it so and keep it so I am (___fill in the blank___), as is best. *Thank You.*

Then recheck, and do additional healing, transmuting, releasing and integrating, as needed.

Tool 3

Throughout The Day As You Wish

Practicing Unconditional LOVE With Ho'oponopono

Based on Self I-dentity Ho'oponopono as taught by Ihaleakala Hew Len. Traditional Ho'oponopono is an ancient Hawaiian method of healing and clearing that requires interaction and cooperation of others. Self I-dentity Ho'oponopono is personal and requires only yourself.

A good introduction to Self I-dentity Ho'oponopono, as taught by Ihaleakala Hew Len, is the book, "Zero Limits", by Joe Vitale and Ihaleakala Hew Len. Self I-dentity Ho'oponopono has been overly commercialized, by some. However, if you get beyond the greed and loss of integrity, by some, and to the original Ho'oponopono, as taught by Ihaleakala Hew Len, you will find it a valuable tool for clearing and healing.

Sometimes the following is taught as, "I Love you. I am sorry. Please forgive me. Thank you." I feel that as you progress it may be best to say, "I Love you. Thank you," with the awareness that at the level of Spirit there is nothing to be sorry for or to be forgiven. Say it with sincerity, whichever ways feels best to you at the time.

Remember that all sources of hurt and pain we have agreed to host manifest as internal self-agreements. Say the following statements mentally. There is no need to project them to the person or situation that hurt, mistreated or angered you. If you feel someone is unforgivable, say them anyway with no thought of the person. Only say them out loud if clearly guided.

"I LOVE You"

Said to "All That Is" and to whomever or whatever has upset you, hurt you, made you sad, made you fearful, even if you have no idea why you are fearful, sad, angry or judgmental.

"Thank You"

Said to "All That Is" and whoever or whatever has upset you, hurt you, made you sad, made you fearful, even if you have no idea why you are fearful, sad, angry or judgmental.

You are thankful for the opportunity to practice "Unconditional Divine LOVE" and clear and heal whatever is of something other than LOVE.

"Clean and Erase as is best"

You are clearing and erasing the memory replaying that has energized hurt, sadness, judgment, attack or anger. The actual memory may remain, however the energy attached to the memory will be healed and released and will no longer affect you. This also often heals, releases and erases any associated trapped or suppressed feelings/emotions. There are often many memories replaying and energizing hurts and beliefs, so realize this is an ongoing practice.

Adapted from *Zero Limits* by Ihaleakala Hew Len and Joe Vitale; pgs 30-32 and from a seminar on Self I-dentity through Ho'oponopono given by Hew Len in 2009

It is vital that we understand what *really* was or still is affecting us.
It was or still is our own beliefs, decisions, agreements and behaviors that manifest our realities.

Practicing Unconditional LOVE Through Prayer

Throughout the day, as you wish.

Great Spirit and Great Spirit Helpers, as are best,
Help and protect (___fill in the blank___), as is best. Send them Your Divine LOVE and LIGHT so that it helps them to open to You as soon as they are ready. *Thank You.*

Tool 4

When You Feel You Are Being Affected, Influenced Or Manipulated By, Or Interfered With By A Person Or Being

Do this if the same person(s)/being(s) repeatedly try to affect, influence, manipulate and/or interfere with you.

Great Spirit and Great Spirit Helpers, as are best,
Do what is best for and what is best with the person(s)/being(s)/entities/energies (___fill in the blank if someone or something specific___) who are trying to interact with me in any way that are of less than Pure LOVE and LIGHT. Do what is best for and what is best with all that are out of harmony with my highest good and well-being.

Remove and heal all being(s)/entities/energies as is best.

Great Spirit and Great Spirit Helpers, as are best,
Surround me with and keep me standing in YOUR LOVE, LIGHT and VIOLET FLAME. *Thank You.*

Great Spirit and Great Spirit Helpers, as are best,
Fill me and all voids with Your LOVE, LIGHT and VIOLET FLAME as is best. *Thank You.*

Tool 5

Relaxation

The Easiest Way To Relax Yourself

"Put the left hand at the base of your spine and the right hand in the curve where your head and neck meet – just hold them there and you will begin to relax. Placing your hands that way connects the positive and negative poles of the nervous system, and the energy flowing back and forth balances the body and calms you down. If you sit awhile like that sometimes, you find you can almost put yourself to sleep. That's a simple way to help yourself relax -- you can even do it at work. If you put the left up top and the right at the bottom, it works the opposite way, it makes you irritable, so be sure the left hand is at the base of the sine and the right hand is at the base of the skull.

You can be most effective if you're Balanced. People who write me often end up with a New Age saying, "Walk in Balance." **But** do they know how to walk in Balance? If your brain is too focused on one side, you may be walking around at an angle yourself. By opening both sides of the brain, then you can walk in Balance.

You may have heard about the left and right hemispheres of the brain. The left side is logical and there's nothing wrong with logic. The right side has a connection with the ethereal, the spiritual aspects of life, and the two sides of the brain must be kept in Balance for you to lead a Balanced life." *

* Bear Heart. *The Wind Is My Mother* (p. 127 and 128*)*

Tool 6

Before Bed

The Thought Extinguishing Exercise

"This night-time exercise, for one, is good for releasing stressful obligations, helping you sleep better and resetting your mental power. It is good for mental emptying and releasing mental control.

You can do this exercise during the day if you feel yourself going into mental overload, **but** for the most part it's designed to do at bedtime to help you enjoy better health and a good night's sleep.

Start by making yourself comfortable, either lying down or sitting. Take a few deep breaths and let your muscles relax. Imagine a warm and comforting campfire in front of you and stare into the flames. Place whatever thoughts come to you into the fire. You can imagine them as having shape and form if you wish. One by one, look at each thought and then see it burn away in the fire, going up in smoke. This will take anywhere from 5 to 20 minutes, depending on how many thoughts come into your mind.

If imagining the fire is a problem for you, you might feel more comfortable picturing yourself standing by a river and letting your thoughts wash downstream. Or, you could stand on a mountain top and let your thoughts be blown away with the wind. Whatever image allows you to release your thoughts so that you feel relaxed and Peaceful is fine.

If any particular thought offers resistance and keeps coming back to you, tell yourself that you do**n't** have to deal with it right then-you can be reminded of it in the morning. Take a deep breath and let it out, mentally affirming that all situations eventually resolve themselves. This might help you let go of a particularly difficult thought. In the world of thought, what makes an imagined outcome turn into a problem is believing that it will happen. Why do that? Let it be. Your mind must empty at night in order to heal." *

* Dr. Mark Laursen. *The Inside-Outside Diet* (p.89 and 90)

Glenn's Comment:
If there is something you feel you must do tomorrow write it down before you go to bed and let go of it for the night. Make a conscious decision at the end of the day to let go of negative and judgmental thoughts and anxieties.

Tool 7

Living In Grace Rather Than Under The Law of Karma

You may say the following as prayers and/or ask if you have already completed the healing. If you have more healing to do, I leave it to you to do your own healing in your own way.

This page is specifically about letting go of 'Karma' and replacing it with 'Grace'. You may believe that you owe debts and remain under the 'Law of Karma', or you may make your will One with God and live under the 'Law of Grace'. Grace is a law, just as karma is a law, however Grace lacks the sting that one can experience from cause and effect.

Suggested ways of bringing one's self under the Law of Grace:

Be kind, noble, selfless. Be willing to assist others without thoughts of reward.

Be happy, joyful, merry, blissful, festive, jolly and cheerful. See the Light Side as often as possible. Turn dark issues to Light. There is another side to every question. Cultivate humor within yourself.

Shift Perception to the positive. See the LIGHT Side.

Be gentle, even when in pain. Give LOVE to the God within everyone's inner self.

Set your ideal and intent toward LOVE. Some laws are personal. Other laws are 'Universal Laws' and are immutable/unchangeable. If your ideal and intent is set toward LOVE none of these laws should separate you from the awareness and benefits of Grace.

Release and let go of those feelings, emotions and memories that would fill you with guilt, judgment and self-judgment. Turn your face to the LIGHT of God always, and the shadows of doubt and fear will fall far behind.

Be creative: All individuals, with all the attributes of body, soul and spirit, are subject to the 'Universal Laws'. As you harmonize with Divine LOVE to do or to accomplish that which is your Creative Influence, realize the difference between the Universal Law of Karma and the Universal Law of Grace. Only the Universal Law of Grace will bring you fully into God's Divine LOVE.

Forgive and LOVE: Only when you forgive and LOVE will you then be forgiven and LOVED. Remember to always forgive and LOVE yourself too.

You may be exercising some of these patterns some of the time. Unless you are consistently following all of them all of the time, you have to admit there is room for improvement.

There Really Are Just Two Choices.

Join God Source in GRACE and LOVE
or
Anything Else.

Tool 8

More Practices, Requests and Prayers

You may want to read this tool quickly once and then come back to use it as prompts for prayer and questions.

Breathe in LOVE and breathe out peace with proper deep breaths for several minutes, several times per day. (With practice it will become automatic and you will begin to always breathe in LOVE and breathe out peace .)

Simply sit in the LOVE 'That I AM' and relax into the heart.

Surrender to the simplicity of living from the 'Heart Space'.

Receive 'Cosmic LOVE', 'which I AM', and allow it to flow through in a seamless 'State of LOVE'.

Rest and be nourished in the Simplicity and the peace which surpasses understanding.

Live and breathe each moment from the Heart with the great LOVE of self and 'All That I AM'.

Release and let go of all the 'stuff', knowing that I AM omniscient, omnipresent, omnipotent and can retrieve any information that may be needed in any given moment. Realize each of us must take responsibility for that which we receive.

Take time to rest. Soak in, absorb and radiate the pure simple frequencies and LOVE of the cosmic energies continually radiating through the universe.

Share 'That Which I AM' with LOVE.

Be ready, willing and open. Ask for the doors to open with utter Divine LOVE, Grace, ease and effortlessness to now bring forth, for fair exchange, "All That I AM'; all that I have to share.

Allow all the programming to simply dissolve and be transmuted in the 'VIOLET FLAME' of God's Infinite Perfection.

Realize and be aware that past, present and future are all here in the center of the present.

Know that true prosperity goes hand-in-hand with peace and LOVE.

Have clarity about whatever the topic may be and be in alignment with 'The Divine Flow', moment to moment.

Let all the stories go, let all the identities go, let all the strategies go and let all the modalities go. You may still sometimes use them when best in the moment, with 'All That I AM' in utter trust as guided.

Let go, relinquish control, think less and *feel* more.
Trust 'All That I AM' more.

Allow all my Helpers of LIGHT and LOVE to bring all of my energies and all of my timelines gathered together in all 'That I AM'.

Gather all my parts and pieces, ‘All That I AM’, into the Heart with LOVE.
The piece that overrides them all:

Be resting in the Heart, with all the LOVE, with all the feeling, with all the vulnerability; with all the openness, flow and creativity that comes through the heart.

Let go of all the tensions deeply held through many cycles of time.

Allow this to trigger a deep, deep, deep relaxation of the physical vehicle.

Refocus in this way so I breath in golden/white opalescent diamond LIGHT and LOVE through the heart and breath out peace.

Bring ‘All That I AM’ into alignment with Great Spirit, ready to move forward with ease and grace in full alignment with that which I AM here to do at this time.

Have a deep trust in ‘All That I AM’, in Creator and in the unfolding of Creation. Let go of any conceptions of what 'reality' is, of what is going on, of what is happening , of what I need to 'do'.

Simply:

Be open to LOVE, to the unfoldment of life and creation, as it continues, breath to breath, moment to moment.

Be in ‘The Divine Flow’ and be utterly grounded.

Be in alignment with my infinite chakras, energy centers and centers of consciousness.

Be in alignment with the ‘Heart of Mother’ in LOVE.

Be in alignment through the ‘Heart of Mother’.

Be in alignment with the infinite spirals of chakras, energy centers and centers of consciousness that represent ‘All That We Are’, in LOVE.

Brought to the attention of the world in a speech by Nelson Mandela.

"Our deepest fear is **not** that we are inadequate

Our deepest fear is that we are powerful beyond measure.

It is our Light, **not** our darkness, that most frightens us.

We ask ourselves, who am I to be brilliant, gorgeous, talented, fabulous?

Actually, who are you **not** to be?

You are a child of God.

Your playing small does**n't** serve the world.

There's nothing enlightened about shrinking so that other people wo**n't** feel insecure around you.

We are all meant to shine, as children do.

We were born to make manifest the glory of God that is within us.

It's **not** just in some of us; it's in everyone.

And as we let our own light shine, we unconsciously give other people permission to do the same.

As we're liberated from our own fear, our presence automatically liberates others."

A Return to Love: Reflections on the Principles of "A Course In Miracles" by Marianne Williamson>

Appendix
Concurrent Healing Techniques

1) **Other Styles Of Prayer.**
2) **Inner Child Healing**: Healing of the feeling, emotional and mental wounds of the inner child, including changed perceptions and integration of the dark side, with forgiveness and LOVE, rather than blame.
3) **Soul Retrieval:** Retrieval of soul pieces ready to integrate. Treatment of fragmented and lost (or stolen) soul parts that keep one from being Spiritually whole. Missing soul fragments create openings in the manifest and unmanifest bodies.
4) **Personal Empowerment Techniques**: Personal empowerment provided by a Spiritual reconnection with one's Highest Self and with The All-Powerful, All-Knowing Creator of the Universe. Feelings of aloneness and separation are replaced with compassion, forgiveness and LOVE.
5) **Meditation and Contemplation**
6) **Nutrition and Eating Habits**
7) **Physical Fitness and Exercise**
8) **Minimizing Damaging Habits**: Smoke less or become a non smoker, limit caffeine, limit carbonated beverages, limit alcoholic beverages, limit refined/processed foods, limit other non-nutritious foods.
9) **Acupuncture**
10) **Hypnosis**
11) **Shamanic Healing**
12) **Energy Healing**
13) **Chiropractic**
14) **Massage and 'Bodywork'**
15) **Training**: Train yourself to recognize your State of Being and your health.
16) **Supplements and Medicines**
17) **Holistic Doctors and Practitioners**
18) **Traditional Western Medicine**

Suggested Reading and Web Sites

Books I have written and Web Site

Two Choices - Divine Love or Anything Else (This Book)

Awareness - A Path To Spiritual and Physical Health and Well-Being

Concepts and Practices of Healing

http://twochoices.net for additional information and FREE PDFs

Dental And Mouth

Elements of Danger: Protect Yourself Against the Hazards of Modern Dentistry by Morton Walker, D.P.M. (can be overwhelming)

<http://www.hugginsappliedhealing.com/>

<http://www.talkinternational.com/toothchart.html> (for interactive tooth to organ chart)

<http://www.flcv.com/indexa.html>

<http://www.secretofthieves.com/tooth-chart/> (an even more detailed tooth to organ chart)

Nutrition

No one nutritional and eating plan is right for everyone. When looked at with a critical eye the following three plans combine for a good basis.

Eat Right For Your Type by Dr. Peter J. D'Adamo
<http://dadamo.com/>

Enter The Zone by Barry Sears, PhD
<http://zonediet.com/zone-diet-overview>

The Metabolic Typing Diet by William Wolcott and Trish Fahey
<http://www.healthexcel.com/>

<http:/FindaSpring.com> (can help you find a natural spring close to you)

Affirmations

You Can Heal Your Life by Louise L. Hay

Memories Replaying

Zero Limits by Ihaleakala Hew Len, PhD and Joe Vitale

A very good introduction to healing and releasing 'Memories Replaying' by practicing Self Identity Ho'oponopono as developed and taught by Morrnah Nalamaku Simeona and Ihaleakala Hew Len. I have been unable to find a web site that is Ihaleakala Hew Lens'. His teachings are very powerful, however many people have commercialized them.

<http://top411.tripod.com/zero-limits-with-hooponopono/dr_ihaleakala_hew_len.html>

(A web page with links to video interviews with Ihaleakala Hew Len)

Trapped/Hidden Feelings, Emotions and Aspects

The Emotion Code by Dr. Bradley Nelson

<http://www.drbradleynelson.com/filters/the-emotion-code/>

Emotional Clearing Process by John Ruskan

<http://www.emclear.com/index.html>\

The Dark Side Of The Light Chasers by Debbie Ford

<http://store.debbieford.com/product_info.php?products_id=9>

Magnets for Healing

<https://www.lyonlegacy.com/learn/behind_science_magnetics.aspx>

The Ringing Cedars Series by Vladimir Megre

This series of books tells of Vladimir's learning from a Siberian recluse named Anastasia.

Some people believe Vladimir Megre has met Anastasia and the book is based on actual events. Some people say it is a work of fiction. Some people even say that there is no such person as Vladimir Megre.

I just found a web site <http://archive.org/advancedsearch.php> that has all 9 books in the series available as FREE downloads in EPUB, MOBI for Kindle and PDF formats. The PDF with text is searchable for words and phrases.

Book 1 *Anastasia* by Vladimir Megre

Book 2 *The Ringing Cedars of Russia* by Vladimir Megre

Book 3 *The Space of Love* by Vladimir Megre

Book 4 *Co-Creation* by Vladimir Megre

Book 5 *Who Are We?* by Vladimir Megre

Book 6 *The Book Of Kin* by Vladimir Megre

Book 7 *The Energy of Life* by Vladimir Megre

Book 8.1 *The New Civilization* by Vladimir Megre

Book 8.2 *Rites of Love* by Vladimir Megre

<http://www.vladimirmegre.com/vladimir_megre_story.php>

<http://www.anastasia.ca/>

Good Information On Muscle Testing

<http://www.holistichealthtools.com/muscle.html>

Excellent Practice (modify for yourself)

Everyday Enlightenment - The Twelve Gateways to Personal Growth by Dan Millman

References

Books

Heart, Bear, & Larkin, Molly. (1996). *The Wind Is My Mother.* New York: The Berkley Publishing Group.

Hew Len, Ihaleakala, & Vitale, Joe. (2007). *Zero Limits*. Hoboken, New Jersey: John Wiley & Sons.

Laursen, Dr. Mark. (2008). *The Inside-Outside Diet.* Tybee Island, Georgia: Natural Body Health.

Williamson, Marianne. (1996). *A Return to Love: Reflections on the principles of "A Course In Miricles"*. New York: Harper Collins Publishers.

Ford, Debbie. (1998). *The Dark Side Of The Light Chasers.* New York: The Berkley Publishing Group.

McKenna, Jed. (2007). *Spiritual Warfare*.No city given: WiseFool Press.

Seminars

Hew Len, Ihaleakala. *Self I-dentity through Ho'oponopono Basic*. IZI LLC. Woodland Hills, CA. Oct 31 and November 1, 2009

About The Author

Glenn Molinari was born in Wilmington, Delaware on April 17, 1948. Until 1954, his family lived in Southern New Jersey, at which time the family moved to the suburbs just outside Wilmington. Glenn served our Country in the Air Force from 1968 to 1972. After having been honorably discharged, he moved back to Delaware and in 1996 moved in with his father on the Eastern Shore of Maryland.

In 1997, Glenn became involved with alternative medicine to address personal health issues that Western Medicine had been unable to diagnose or to cure. While Glenn was learning about alternative therapies and the Body/Mind/Spirit connections, he remained at his father's side as caregiver until 2007. He moved to Cornville, Arizona in 2008, where he resides today.

Glenn continues his interest in choosing Divine LOVE, practicing awareness and alternative healing modalities. He continues to share with those interested.

I hope you have found this helpful.

If you wish, you may contact Glenn Molinari

telephone: 1 (928) 300-6202

email: glenn@twoChoices.net

Web Site: http://twoChoices.net

www.ingramcontent.com/pod-product-compliance
Lightning Source LLC
LaVergne TN
LVHW070145110826
845147LV00002B/328

* 9 7 8 0 9 8 5 4 7 8 4 1 4 *